MW01122814

1

Margott Schuerings

Blow Your Mind

-

The Mystery of Michael Jackson and Sathya Sai Baba

1st English Edition, 2016
(translated from German, 1999, 2009)
ADWAITA

The German Library - CIP-unit recording
A track record for this publication
is available at the German library.

Schuerings, Margott:
Blow Your Mind -
The Mystery of Michael Jackson and Sathya Sai Baba /
Margott Schuerings
1st English edition, 2016
Hohenpeissenberg, Adwaita-Verlag
First published in German, Adwaita-Verlag with the title:
Das Mysterium von Michael Jackson und Sathya Sai Baba,
1999, 2nd edition 2009

Translation: Margott Schuerings
English editor: Alex Knight

Copyright: 2016 ADWAITA-Verlag
www.adwaita-verlag.de

EAN: Paperback 978934281059
Cover: BoD

Content   page

Foreword 1st and 2nd German Edition, 1999, 2009

Since 1992 I had the dream of seeing Michael Jackson and Sathya Sai Baba together on a stage. Many years I've been fascinated by their message and was studying their words and lyrics. Only the imagination of a joint performance on stage fills my heart with joy and enthusiasm. That day will be a leap for humanity which is of much more importance than the first step of man on the moon.

When I talk to people about this vision they look at me without understanding and I feel that some think that I am a little bit insane. Some few wanted to know more and thus we passed exciting hours lifting the veil of the mystery of Michael Jackson and Sathya Sai Baba.

One thing is for sure: Both are unique, each one in his own manner. It is not easy to express this uniqueness in words because it is located on a level where human language does not yet have the fitting vocabulary - or which perhaps will be located forever beyond words.

For this book I chose these two; they are not chosen Ones. And I want to stress explicitly that I don't say that Michael Jackson and Sathya Sai Baba know each other; I state that I have no knowledge of a connection of the two on a physical level. I describe their connection that is exemplary for all living beings and which was called by Ken Wilber the level of "One Taste."

I want to share my discovery with all those who are seeing with the heart and who are on a journey with the goal to recognize that they only travel from self to Self.

The dream continues...this time it is a waking dream.

With love to all co-travelers ... Margott Schuerings, September 1999

Foreword to the 1st English Edition, 2016

The research for this book started in 1992, the results were published in 1999 under the title "The Mystery of Michael Jackson and Sathya Sai Baba".

Since then more and more people are ready and willing to grasp the message and to realize that it has nothing to do with the person Michael Jackson and the persona of Sathya Sai Baba, but that it deals with the mystery, which will reveal itself to everyone, who starts on the journey from self to Self. Michael Jackson and Sathya Sai Baba both conveyed the same message, at time with the same words.

Truth cannot only be found in religions and churches, but everywhere, where there are open ears and especially open hearts ready to listen ...

This book exclusively concentrates on the message, the spirit, consciousness and the essence of the work of these two embodiments during their time on earth. The author has no knowledge and is not interested in the question, if they ever met on the physical plane or if there was any other form of relationship between the two.

For the purpose of this book this knowledge is absolutely expendable. Period!

Their message is equally valid now as it was in 1999 and 2009 (1st and 2nd German edition), which everyone who is ready and able to read with the heart can prove for himself.

Thank you all you lovely beings ... I love you more
Margott Schuerings, August 2016

1.   Diagnosis

Humanity is suffering a terrible disease which has been spreading over the whole globe for centuries and has still, even now, not stopped before any border. People of all ages, races, nationalities, classes and religions are suffering from the same disease. As of yet, academic science has not discovered this disease and not diagnosed it.

How is it possible that a disease that is rampant throughout the whole globe has not yet been discovered even after centuries?

Academic science is itself most badly affected. It cannot see the beam in its own eye and does not believe the ones who have sufficient distance to themselves to see it, because that would mean to drop their faith and aspiration in the infallibility of academic science - and thus it's claim to power would be forfeited.

And yet this disease is identified and has been known for a long time. Holy men, wise men, mystics and world teachers refer to it relentlessly. But nobody listens. They are heard, but not listened to. What type of strange disease is this so many people are denying, which nobody accepts to be true?

It is the "collective amnesia" of mankind, the complete loss of memory, the full blackout.

And what is it that man has forgotten? What does he not remember? What is it he does not know?

These are the answers to the questions:

Who am I?

Who are you?

Where did we come from?

Where are we going?

What's it all about?

With these words begins Michael Jackson's poem "ARE YOU
listening?" (in: *Dancing the Dream, 1992*), with exactly the questions
which seekers of truth have been asking for ages, the questions for our
origin, our source, our identity, our purpose, our goal.

Sathya Sai Baba confirms:

In Vedanta man is encouraged to inquire: Who am I?
Sanathana Sarathi, 08/1997

Vedanta means "end of the Veda." The Veda are holy scriptures and
revelations whose origin is unknown and about which research dates to
long before the year 1500 BC. In reality they may be much older, possibly
ageless. Veda means "knowledge." What is knowledge? We will ponder on
this question later.

And what about the disease of memory loss? One does only not search
for something when one does not notice that something was forgotten or
lost. When one does not notice a loss it seems that the thing was not so
valuable, because valuable things we will keep in mind and start
immediately to search for after a loss. What sort of loss is this that misses
our attention and that we don't even care about? Is it really that we are so
indifferent about our origin? Are we not interested in where we come
from, in where our home is? Don't we want to know from where we
originate?

The state of modern man is absurd and crazy, as is shown by the
following example. If we ask a traveler on the road, "Where do you come
from?" and he is unable to give an answer, we think about him as a
strange, wacko, and rightly so. When we continue to ask: "Who are you?"
and he is again stuck for an answer , we see him as a candidate for a
psychiatric ward. But exactly that is the state of man today. He is unable to
answer the questions, "Where do you come from?" and "Who are you?,"

and even worse, he has not even a clue to ask these questions. He is wandering the earth, he is invading the farthest corners of jungles and deserts, he is climbing the highest mountains, diving into the deepest depths of the oceans, he is landing on the moon and is reaching to the planets, but has not yet started on the journey to the Self; he is not even interested in it. The wise Nisargadatta Maharaj advises every traveler: "Know yourself, the rest will follow." (p. 17)

Man is equipped with a memory as well as the ability to forget....The tragedy is that he has forgotten the most important and crucial thing of his earthly career - the key to happiness and liberation, his true name and identity. Man cannot afford to forget who he is and to what purpose he has come. He should know the answers to the questions: Who are you? Who am I? Where do I go? Where do I come from?
Sathya Sai Baba speaks, Vol. 5 (new ed.) 14th of July 1965(* see p. 127)

And there is good news. The century-long deep slumber is coming to an end. Sociologist James Redfield describes the "collective awakening of humanity from a century-long 'weltanschauung's dream'" in the prophecies and the vision of Celestine (1994, 1996, 1998), "where we were wandering the world intently with blinders." We developed the scientific method and did not realize that it served as an alibi to hide and suppress our insecurity and fear of real life. "In a sort of collective obsessiveness we dug into material issues and the scientists we charged fell for centuries into the trap they had created themselves." (Redfield 1998, p. 57-58*)

Now you are running around and asking everybody you meet: 'Who are you?', but seldom do you look inward and ask yourself: 'Who am I?"
Sathya Sai Baba Speaks, Vol 6, (new ed.), chap 44

2.   Reminder

We want to listen to the messages of two embodiments on our planet, who are not suffering from this horrible disease of "amnesia" - the earthly star Michael Jackson and the heavenly star Sathya Sai Baba. Michael Jackson tells us of "Two Birds":

Two birds fly through the air

One's song drops like crystal from the sky

...the other spreads wings of invisibility...

It's easy to guess which bird I am,

but they'll never find you.

Unless...

Michael Jackson, Two Birds, Dancing the Dream

It lies at the heart of Michael Jackson that people will find the second bird, and that will also be the theme of this book. What is so difficult about finding it? Isn't it said: Who searches will find? And aren't we all searchers? The problem is that we are searching in the wrong places, in the wrong manner and that we don't really know **what** we are looking for. We are searching in the outer world, we are searching with the five senses, we are searching and searching. To finally find the "second bird" we have to change the direction of our search, we have to explore the inner worlds, we have to search with the heart, not with the physical eyes.

What has this search to do with our disease? What is the healing for the "collective amnesia"? The word "healing" is derived from the meaning "whole," German "heil." The German word "Heiland" has the same root and means "Savior."

13

One who is healed from a disease is saved, is whole, is in order. In our society, increasing numbers of people are aspiring for healing and salvation, with even our health system being more a disease system with the purpose to annihilate the manifestation of a disease in the physical body. The goal is the absence of disease. Absence of disease is yet not presence of health, in the same way as absence of poverty does not mean presence of richness, or absence of depression does not mean presence of joy. An increasing number of people are no longer satisfied with the removal of disease, but they are aspiring for health, wholeness and salvation.

The healing of the "collective amnesia" is remembering, re-membering of who I am, where I come from and where I am going. Healing happens when the remembrance of my identity and my origin is returning....Man wants to control the outer things, is searching for security, wants always to know what is coming next and does not realize that his inner world is full of compulsions, conditioned emotions, inclinations and inborn tendencies. He clings to the elusive security of habits and floats in the stream of life. In relation to his own life and source the non-reminder turns off his pondering. He does not reflect, does not contemplate, does not put on his thinking, does not think about things that happened, but prefers to worry, to bother about things that did not yet happen and to plan what he will do after it happens. In other words, he is preoccupied, pre occupied, occupied with possibilities and the future, not realities and the present, bringing sorrow instead of joy, is blaming himself without understanding that what happened is a necessary lesson to learn, not something to avoid, and that everything we encounter in our life is a gift to return to wholeness and be whole in the here and now. Only being present in the here and now enables us to create a better future. Instead the non-reminder continues to sleep the sleep of "Sleeping Beauty," dreaming his nightmares, and tries at times to change his nightmares to pleasant dreams. But it continues being

14

a dream. He does not recognize that he is sleeping and should awaken to deal with reality and know his origin and purpose.

This is really strange conduct when we consider that the urge to know one's origin is innate in man. We can observe again and again that people who don't know their physical parents feel the urge to start the search for them, to know where they come from, where their roots are.
When the longing to know the physical parents is innately so irresistible, why are we then so uninterested in the search for our spiritual origin? Our physical parents are like us, a river, and we are the tributary river. But where is the wellspring? Where is the home of our soul?
The one who wants healing from the disease of "collective amnesia," who wants to restore order, wholeness, completeness, holiness, instead of being cut off, being torn inside, at odds with oneself, not okay, who wants to overcome suffering, to look through, to scrutinize the mundane and the profane things, has to train his memory until he will re-member everything he once knew. A famous Zen koan says: "Show me your original face, the face you had before your parents were born." (Wilber, 1999, p. 366*)

There is no change necessary to heal the loss of memory, but we need only make whole what was broken, to put together what was separated. It is a matter of putting the parts again at their hereditary place. Sathya Sai Baba describes this process in a metaphor:

There was a little boy who succeeded to find a way to the office of his father. Normally it is not allowed the little boy to enter it, because there are treasured some very valuable documents, so the door is kept closed. But one day it happened that the door was only left ajar and also the window was open, so that an air draft entered the room. The boy saw the open door and entered. And exactly that moment an important document was swept across by the air draft from the table and landed on the floor. It was a very rare and very old map of the world, a beautiful colored map, where each color stood for a different country. The boy saw this wonderful piece of paper. He took it and looked at it and started to fold it in

15

one direction and the other direction...oh it was so wonderful to play with it, to make a little boat of it, then a hat and then a house. But the old map could not stand to be folded so often and soon it broke into two pieces, then into four pieces and then into eight and even more pieces of different colors. The little boy was very pleased by the turn of matters...now he had more things to play with and soon the whole world was broken to pieces.

The father entered and realized that his son had played with the world and that he had succeeded in breaking the whole world to pieces. The father was very concerned: "Son look what you have done. You broke the world to pieces." But nevertheless he was his son. He was only a little boy and really innocent. He happened to sleepwalk in something and started to play. So the father could not really be angry with him. But the world was now torn to pieces and so the father decided to teach his son an important lesson. He said: "Son you should not have broken the world to pieces. Look, here I am giving you adhesive tape and you will put everything together again. When you put it all together again your father will feel better and you will feel better too."

No matter how much he tried the little boy did not know how to put the world together again. There were simply too many pieces and he could not figure out how they would fit together. But then came an air draft and it happened that one of the pieces was turned to the back side. There on the back side he could recognize a human eye. What a surprise! He turned another piece to the back and saw a hand on the other side. And then he saw a nose on another piece and on another a foot and then a head and then a shoulder and soon he had turned all pieces to the back and saw all the different parts of a human body. Now, even a little boy knows what a human body looks like. Now he had a puzzle which he could put together. And soon he had completed the whole human being. After using the tape to hold all pieces together he noticed that he now had the beautiful picture of a complete human being in front of him. And when he turned the whole thing on the other side, the whole world was to his great joy put together again.

Sathya Sai Baba, cit. in Drucker: Ich bin, p. 10f*

The remembrance of the original will return when we put together the puzzle, when we focus the torn and distorted mind on the One and Whole and break and tame the analytical mind. Then the memory of the whole picture which is lying in the deeper levels of our soul, which are located beyond mind, can emerge and reach our consciousness. "Plato himself says that we were once whole, but neglecting to remember - amnesis - allows us to lapse from this wholeness. And we will recover from our fragmentation when we *remember* who and what we are in reality." (Wilber, 1999, p. 360*)

The only sinfall of mankind is that he forgot who he is. As he does not know who he is, he is not able to come into his inheritance. As he does not know who he is he does not know his birthright. Instead he believes that he is a sinner. That is his error. "His reality did not change only because it was forgotten. Forgiveness is the means by which we will remember." (Course in miracles, Foreword, p. xxi)

3.   The Eye of the Heart

Wholeness and healing reveal themselves when we open the inner eye,
look through the shell and manifestation of the material, and see through
to the core to reach the essence, the being. The outer eyes don't reach to
these depths. The essence can only be perceived with the inner eye.
Antoine de Saint Exupéry reveals this wisdom in the parable of the rose
and the fox:

"Adieu, said the fox to the little prince. Here is my secret. It's simple: You
only see good with the heart. The essential is invisible for the eyes....Man
has forgotten this truth....But you may not forget it." *(de Saint Excupéry,
1992, p. 98*)*

   The fox confronts the reasoning of the mind, of logic, and the wisdom
that is directed outside with the vision directed inside. This vision will
reveal the wholeness of man and put the world together. The world and
man are like the two sides of a medal, inextricably linked to each other,
and each side will suffer the fate of the other side.

   When man has recognized that he is whole and in one piece, then he is
redeemed and holy. May the parting of the ways cause screaming with
horror when they hear words like "holy" and "redeemed." It only shows
how far humanity absented itself from reality and truth and how strong is
the resistance against the essence and the self. Only on the level of
essence, being, of human nature, is understanding possible. Words and
language are only signs and instruments for man to reach the level of
essence.

   Why is understanding with words impossible?
   Words are a priori void shells which have no meaning. The one who
uses a word is giving it its whole meaning. Some aspects of the meaning
of different people overlap due to the collective experiences or the

collective trance (Wolinsky, 1993*), which humanity is actually undergoing. But the meanings are not identical, because everyone fills a word with the totality of his experiences with this word and on this planet there are no two people with identical experiences. Let's take the word "chair." Besides the fact that in a certain cultural and social environment everybody understands that it stands for an object on which one can sit, this word has aspects of meaning which originate from the experiences of both speaker and listener with this word. Therefore it is about conscious and unconscious aspects of the meaning. The one who chooses a word fills it with his own subjective meaning, the expression. The listener fills it with his own subjective meaning, the impression. Expression and impression are not identical, because no two people give a hundred percent identical meaning to a word. There is an intersection with matching meaning and there is the remaining quantity of the speaker and the remaining quantity of the listener. Every word is afflicted with associations, thoughts and feelings which are different for everyone. Therefore there is no perfect understanding between men by words, because the associations, emotions and thoughts of people to the thing indicated hamper a clear vision of reality. The associations pretend that we are able to understand that for which the words stands. In reality we understand nothing. Neither the perceived nor the thought nor the felt has a meaning in itself. Only when we go beyond words and open up to the reality beyond words, can the essence reveal itself. The truth which can be found by steering towards the inside reveals by itself when we let go of, release, the meaning which originated from the outer sight.

Human evolution is directed unceasingly towards the identity of expression and impression. Only when expression and impression are identical are perfect understanding and comprehension possible. In the actual state of evolution of mankind, identity of expression and impression is very rare. We will rarely find it in words but only in "silent understanding."

The reader also will decide by himself if he will fill my words, my expression with his own meaning, and then use it for his own purposes, or if he is willing to see with the heart and then figure out what I want to express so that it matches most possibly with his impression and thus speaks One Voice and the meaning is in harmony, is One Sound.

It doesn't matter if the reader chooses controversy or reconciliation, as both have their function and purpose in the cosmic game or drama, and thus I hand over my gift to the world, like a gardener who entrusts the seed to the soil. The reader is responsible for whether he lets the seed fall on stony or fertile ground, if he will water the seed or let it dry up. I was flirting with the idea of delivering in this book also the rebuttal of this book, but finally decided to let the opinions that differ on this question fight the battle by themselves, because in the moment you fight against a thing you fight against yourself. Every contradiction is capable of reconciliation, because in the end it was created for the purpose of reconciliation for us to realize that there is only "One Son" and that "the Father and the Son are One." The words "son" and "reconciliation" have the same root in German ("Sohn," "Versöhnung"). But instead of searching for reconciliation man is following the path of division, because he is following his torn mind instead of his heart and his soul. Words are interpreted controversially by a torn mind. Twisted and limited minds deliver twisted and limited meanings. Due to his insane mind man is limiting himself, because he is what he thinks. He is not even capable of recognizing that he does not understand.

The categorical statement "Cogito ergo sum," "I think therefore I am," of the philosopher Descartes from the 17th century, about whom it is said that he gave modern science critical independence, is a fatal dogma, originated by the myth that being is bound to form and by the deep-rooted desire of man to hold on to something, to hold something. Thus were created ties, fetters and chains, which continue today to tie scientists and science - and in a double sense - they are confined to it and they are tied by it. Dogma impedes that freethinker and lateral thinker are listened to and those who are reaching to a level beyond thinking have one's say.

When man would first learn to love instead of analyzing and judging the world and humanity with his mind, he could find the door to eternity, because only thoughts born from love can mirror reality, which is unchangeable and eternal. Michael Jackson challenges us all in his hymn "Childhood" to revert the order of judgment and love:

Before you judge me try hard to love me.
Michael Jackson, Childhood, HIStory

Is he relating to himself? Or does he - representative - express an eternal law? Plato's teaching of the ideas postulates an imagination a priori. This "does not enter man from the outside, but he remembers it as something that he is already possessing, but did forget. The realization of the idea is recognition (anámnesis)." (DTV Lexikon) This very first idea has its origin in a realm which comes after thinking and is located beyond the mind, which is incomprehensible by terms, concepts or words, but can be experienced by insight and awareness and reveals itself directly without words. Michael Jackson points to this realm in his hymn "Heal the World":

There is a place in your heart and I know that it is love.
Michael Jackson, Heal the World, HIStory

The one who goes to see this place knows...and this knowing can never be shattered by anything because it is absolute, eternal and unchangeable. "I know that I know nothing" is the first realization of every human being who has made the first step on the path to true knowledge. "Know nothing" means all the facts, theories and concepts which were collected under the name "science" and are in reality only the collected compendium of not-knowledge, ignorance.

21

Academic science claims a degree for itself which it does not deserve because it knows nothing, but it constructs a reality. I don't deny the value and the achievements of scientific research and cognition, its observances and deductions. Academic science has contributed eminently to better the quality of life of man, but at the same time it has contributed to the diminution of true knowledge because it usurped the place of "knowledge." It should not claim the title "science," because it does not deal with "knowing" but with theories, hypotheses and proving them as well as conclusions due to statistical relations and mathematical models. To every hypothesis there is a counterhypothesis and they can all be proven. It is characteristic for material science that every theory and every conviction takes in its tow the corresponding proofs. Those who have the opposite opinion shall surrender to the burden of proof. Thus follows a permanent back-and-forth between representatives of different paradigms, a tug-of-war of contraries, and each side tries to succeed in pulling the rope to its own side. If everyone were honest with himself , he would recognize academic science for what it is - conviction or belief, as for example the past belief that the earth is flat and the center of the cosmos - it is really a twisted world we have created.

The terms "science" and "knowledge" should remain reserved for the knowledge and the science that deserve this title, that means for the knowledge which creates certainty, which comes from the source, which springs from the origin, which is eternal and unchangeable and does not change with time or adapts to the "zeitgeist." Everything that changes cannot be knowledge, Veda. Something is true or not true, but it cannot be true today and untrue tomorrow. There is only one truth and it should be the duty of a realm which calls itself science to explore and find this truth. And everyone is called to be a part of this duty. To be an expert in this realm there are no academic titles required and not even a worldly formation, but instead nobleness of the heart.

Jesus got the point and praises the father, "because you have hidden these things from the wise and learned, and revealed them to the little children." *Matthew 11:25*

And Paul writes to the Corinthians: "For it is written, I will destroy the wisdom of the wise, and I will bring to nothing the understanding of the prudent....For after that in the wisdom of God the world by wisdom knew not God, it pleased God by the foolishness of preaching to save them that belief." *1 Cor. 1. 19,21*

Man has to make the decision to set off the path of wisdom - not of material pseudo wisdom - to be able to receive this "propagation." Gary Zukav calls this path the vertical path, as opposed to the horizontal path *(Zukav, 1990).* Also Paul Tillich talks about the lost vertical dimension. To again find this education is needed, education of character, education of the heart, education of the one, not to pride oneself of oneself or to conceit oneself to be someone, but in the sense that the education is directed inward and focused on the One instead of outward and on the Outside.

Goethe indicates the difference: "One can be taught by society, but one can only be inspired in solitude" *(Thought of the Day, CNN, 3rd of Feb. 1998).* Inspiration means to be filled by pneuma, by Spirit, by SPIRIT. Inspiration happens when the mind, the thinking, is void of concepts, imaginations, ideas and appearances, so that it can be filled with SPIRIT.

The theories, constructs and concepts that are established by material science, are convictions and assumptions, but not knowledge. Material science is a system of beliefs, which scientists are devoted to and for which they are looking for devotees - that is the mission of science. There is no difference to religions, which are belief systems too and looking for devotees. i don't want to condemn systems of belief - not of science nor religion- but only clarify that we are dealing with beliefs and not with knowledge. Everybody is free to decide if and what he wants to believe, in

23

science and also in religion. But everybody should be aware and admit that it is about belief and not about knowledge.

Systems of belief have an important function for an immature man and can be helpful on his life's journey, as long as he is far from the purpose of the Self, and nobody has the right to take these helps away from him. But someday man will recognize that he is devoted to a system of beliefs and that he is lacking the knowledge necessary to assist him in his distress. The title "knowledge" should be reserved to things that we experienced directly, underwent and witnessed ourselves and explored inside. Nothing which was experienced and witnessed by someone else can be knowledge for me. i can acknowledge the experiences of others and then try to make the same experience to finally know myself. Yet the result of my research is unpredictable and i cannot decide on it and not know in advance. The result will only show up after the experience and exploration. Only when i made the experience myself will i know, will i have knowledge.

There are sufficient examples in history that researchers headed off to disprove a hypothesis with the result that they recognized the truth and thus had knowledge. The parapsychologists Dr. Karlis Osis and Dr. Erlendur Haraldsson for example headed off to India to prove that the greatest scientist of all times, Sathya Sai Baba, was a charlatan, and came to the conclusion that he was living proof of the fact that material science knows nothing, and that stand only at the beginning of the discovery what is recorded in the book of the Mystery of Life. Sathya Sai Baba does not obey the laws of material science, but transcends them all. Similar were the experiences of the well-known journalist Russy Kursheed Karanjia, editor of "BLITZ," a tabloid published in India with approximately three million readers, when he interviewed Sathya Sai Baba in 1976, to "cook his goose." He was put right because all the questions he intended to ask him were answered in the interview of two and a half hours before he could

24

bring himself to even ask only one question *(Karanjia, 1994)*. He had to admit that Sathya Sai Baba was all-knowing.

Little children can teach us best what knowing is. When they are asked wherefrom they know certain things, they will answer: "Because I simply know it," and want to say by this that they have experienced the thing. For such knowledge there are not needed justifications or reasons. True knowledge cannot be justified because justification is a function of the mind, while true knowledge is located in a realm beyond mind. How could the mind justify something which is beyond its reach, whose reason it cannot outreach? We need another instrument as the mind for the search for our Self. As Jesus already told us: "Truly I tell you unless you change and become like little children, you will never enter the kingdom of heaven." *(Matthew 18:3)*

The dilemma of modern man is: He builds in his mind, on thinking and reason, and does not notice that he is thereby sealing his narrowness and forfeits his power of discrimination. Like a fool he relies on his mind, believes himself to be the "crown of creation" and misses SPIRIT.

What has all this to do with Michael Jackson and Sathya Sai Baba? Patience!

Patience is the first virtue which we need on our journey - the purpose of a journey is not understood with the first step. The purpose of a journey only becomes apparent when we have reached the goal, when we travel with the heart and when we travel to the heart and - what is most decisive - when we travel ourselves instead of reading the travel report. Everything else is only a foretaste. It is similar to the description of the delicious taste of a fruit. The knowledge about the delicacy only ensues when we have tasted it ourselves.

Our journey shall be one of the heart, because only then understanding is possible. Sathya Sai Baba often alerts us: *There is only one language - the language of the heart.*

In the language beyond words impression and expression can be in unison. Michael Jackson was welcomed in this language by the aborigines in Australia and New Zealand, whereby it was proved that all humans are brothers and sisters.

"They greeted us as brothers even though they didn't speak our language."

Michael Jackson, Moonwalk, p. 106

They were not masters of the language of words, but of a universal language. Michael Jackson became aware of the limitedness of the world that is perceived by the physical senses in his encounters in Japan and China.

"China and Japan were places that helped me grow because these countries helped me understand there was more to life than the things you could hold in your hand or see with your eyes."

Michael Jackson, Moonwalk, p. 106

The bible complains about the inability of man to see and to hear, when he closes his heart.
"Hear this, you foolish and senseless people, who have eyes but do not see, who have ears, but do not hear." *Jeremiah 5:21*

Ken Wilber cites the philosopher Bonaventura who taught us "that man disposes of three types of cognition, of three eyes," as he called it: the eye of the flesh,...the eye of the mind,...and the eye of contemplation....these correspond to the three realms of being, as described by the Philosophia

Perennis, the Eternal Philosophy, as called by Leibniz: the gross (fleshly and material), the subtle (mental and emotional) and the causal (transcendental and contemplative). *Wilber, 1997, p. 98 German ed., 1999, p. 362**

Also psychotherapist Phyllis Krystal indicates the necessity to include the heart when we want to change this world. "...the balance in the world has to be restored by reactivating the heart. But it is up to the individual to effect the changes in the world." *Krystal, 1995, p. XIII**

"If you would have looked straight in my eyes and felt my heart, you would have recognized me...How can somebody know someone when he does not know himself?" asked Merlin, the mysterious seer and magician from the saga around King Arthur. *Kübler, 1996, p. 33**

Adalbert Stifter bequeathed us the knowledge about the meaning of the heart in his report about the solar eclipse of 8th of July 1842: "...mind is already triumphing that he has calculated God's splendor and setup of the heavens....the event comes...but see God gave man also something for the heart with him, what we did not know before and what is a million times more valuable than mind can grasp and calculate: he gave him the word - I am - I am not because of these bodies and this manifestation, but because your heart is telling it to you shivering in this moment and because this heart is sensing great even shivering." *Esotera, 8/1999**

And Goethe puts it in the way of Faustus: "When you don't feel it you will not catch it, when it does not come from the soul and does not urge the hearts of every listener with its primal powerful complacence." *Goethe, Faustus, Night, p. 534-537*

And the result from all this is that one can only know when one knows oneself. This challenge we already found above the portal of the Greek temple in Delphi where we could read the inscription: "Know yourself".

Whoever is curious to find his Self may follow the two signs and tour guides, Michael Jackson and Sathya Sai Baba, on the journey to the Self.

And then he will probably say at the end of the journey, I have known Michael Jackson and Sathya Sai Baba, because I have known my Self. To start on this journey one has to be free from giddiness and elevate himself above the usual, as our two guides are "Two Birds" who will at times carry us off high in the air, to again drop us gently on the ground.

I hear and I forget
I see and I remember
I act and I understand
Confucius, cit. CNN, Thought of the day, 26st Feb. 1998

The only thing I am asking from you is a heart filled with love....The form of the Lord can only be perceived with the eye of unconditional love or with the eye of wisdom, but never with the eye of sensual activity.
Sathya Sai Baba Speaks, Vol. 2*

4.   HIStory

"Michael Jackson is the most famous mortal under the sun. He is also the most abused....In the myth Michael Jackson manifests something which has the finger on the pulse. But social scientists and cultural critics are speechless. They are the only ones whose attention Michael Jackson could not yet catch. They leave one of the most remarkable occurrences of modern civilization to the tabloids." (Ebmeier, p. 7*). That is the beginning of the only book, until 1999, published in German about the Earth Star, who at the transition from the second to the third millenium proposes a conundrum and questions.

At the opposite side of the globe lives the Heaven Star Sathya Sai Baba. Both belong to the extraordinary, incomprehensible and shrouded mystery of the millenium.

Elizabeth Taylor, who has been a friend to Michael Jackson for many years, says about him: "He is not really of this planet. He is filled with deep emotions that create an unearthly, special, innocent, childlike, wise man that's Michael Jackson." *(Dancing the Dream, Introduction)*

Not even the greatest scientist can understand Me by the categories he is accustomed to.
Sathya Sai Baba, cit. by Rodrigo, p. 167*

It is much easier to dismiss Michael Jackson's world of fantasy with malicious gossip than to understand it with empathy, says Jay Cocks in "Time." (March 1984) The world press - from the tabloids to so-called serious journalism - has chosen the simple way to deal with Michael Jackson. It does not bother to use the five senses and even less the sixth and seventh. It ignores the truth about Michael Jackson, because that would push the boundaries of its prejudices and power of imagination and create awareness of the limits of mind. For all those who don't reduce people to their noses, the veil can be unveiled a little bit.

Nearly six billion people know Michael Jackson and yet only a handful have had a glimpse of his message and know what he is moved by, what he imparted and what is the real meaning of his artwork. There is a big gap between the expression of the artist and the impression of the public. Nearly everyone knows his name and his music, but few people - besides the fans - know his lyrics and films, and even fewer his book "Moonwalk." His "Poems and Thoughts" with the title "Dancing the Dream," published in 1992, are nearly unknown in the year 1999. In the meantime this work of art has won many readers. Unfortunately the translation published in German in 1992 covers only the surface and is full of mistranslations and misses the inner meaning of the message - due to judgment and prejudice - because until 1999 nobody took the trouble to analyze Michael Jackson's work in the same way as it is naturally done with other works like that of Hermann Hesse, Goethe and Shakespeare. If we would treat Shakespeare as Michael Jackson *is* treated, he would be trivialized with translations like: "Existence or not existence that is the question" and not with: "To be or not to be that is the question."

Michael Jackson's work is reduced by limited thinking to their own limits and is distorted beyond all recognition by twisted minds. Thereby Michael Jackson's message is profound and healing, at the same time stirring and calming. How is he perceived by people who met him and know him up close and personal?

He is patient and caring --- he is unbelievably strong...warm and natural.
Debbie Jackson Rowe, OK magazine, 11th of April 1997

He is what the French call a "monstre sacre," a holy monster - someone who is absolutely unique.
Gregory Peck, actor

When I first met him it was really love at first sight. When you get to know Michael, you understand his nature of charisma....He looks at the world with the innocent eyes of a child. *Sophia Loren, actress, www.mjfriendship. de*

He is probably the most famous person in the planet. God help him! When Michael Jackson sings it is with the voice of angels, and when his feet move you can see God dancing. *Bob Geldof, Singer*

What is a genius? What is a living legend? What is a megastar? Michael Jackson - that's all. And just when you think you know him, he gives you more. *Elizabeth Taylor, actress*

To Michael Jackson, with appreciation for the outstanding example you have set for the youth of America and the World.
Ronald Reagan, ex-president of the United States, 14th of May 1984

He is the greatest...I mean if I tried to compare him say with Gene Kelly or even Fred Astaire or something like that I would do him an injustice because the thing that makes Michael great is his own style and his own originality.
Hermes Pan, choreographer of Fred Astaire, 1988

You wanna see the boy next door?...Don't go to see Michael Jackson because he ain't the boy next door.
Sammy Davis Jr., entertainer

To work with him as a partner in the film (Ghosts) was one of the greatest experiences in my life.
Stan Winston, film director, www.mjam.com

I was a fan of Michael and have been it, but today I also admire Michael as a human being. *Jimmy Jam, producer, Black & White magazine no. 19/1997*

One of the rare critics who tried seriously to understand Michael Jackson is the Australian Jan Molly Meldrum:

"The greatest entertainer was from earliest childhood a superstar...and 'superstardom'" is a hellish thing, if you want to match with it. Nobody has been there on top for so long as he, and most of those who get there fall down shortly afterwards....Stage stars live in a very, very different world. As long as we have heard, he had a father who abused him and forced him to rehearse, to rehearse, to rehearse, to record, to record, to record, while other children were playing outside with their friends.

His life was unique. There are a handful child stars who managed to take their career to the adult world. Precious few could deliver on their promise, even fewer stayed in front and only one stayed at the top, and that is Michael....Imagine never being able to go out on the street to buy a paper or magazine without a mob of people following you - or even worse.

How would you feel if every time you were seen together with someone else the person in question were considered as you wife or husband?"

Michael may look strange to the world, but I bet that the world looks equally strange to Michael."
J. M. Meldrum, music critic (www.mjifc.com in 1999, no longer available*)

Since the mid-nineties Michael Jackson's music reached a new level. He says about his album HIStory:

Know, the new songs are quite different. They...come from the heart, they are myself. They are no more my songs, I have the feeling they now belong to everyone.

Michael Jackson, HIStory Museum, Sony Homepage (no longer available)

How does that fit together, "they are myself" and "they now belong to everyone"? Many people believe that HIStory is the story of Michael Jackson. In a certain way yes, but only in a certain way. The title of the album is not "My story" and not "His story," but HIStory. Scientists so far have avoided the subject of Michael Jackson, understandably enough because he is not approachable by scientific analysis and does not fit into any system. He is not graspable and not comprehensible and cannot be placed in the usual categories. What shall we do with someone who cannot be classified? He is put aside and then dealing with easier things follows. But as Michael Jackson cannot be overlooked for a long time he cannot be put aside permanently, and as modern man has taken the task of putting everything in the world into drawers, the world press - the tabloids and serious journalism seldom in unison - attended to the matter of Michael Jackson, or better, they had a real go at Michael Jackson. For years the world press has been preoccupied with three nose operations - because there is nothing more important in life - or they've been inventing things that leave the reader, hearer and looker open-mouthed and leave them behind for the next round of "have you already heard?" Michael Jackson himself sees very clearly that in reality nobody is really interested.

Don't you black or white me ...

They're throwing me in a class with a bad name ...

Don't you wrong or right me ...

They don't really care about us.

Michael Jackson, They don't care about us, HIStory album.

Modern man thinks the myths of ancient times are outdated, but on the other hand it is difficult for him to leave things he does not understand the way they are, and starts putting new myths around them. Sathya Sai Baba mentions the reasons:

And here...some journals are spreading all kinds of lies about how things went for me. Without any shame they print their despicable fictions and express thereby their malice and envy on the lowermost level. Naturally such slander is experienced by all who transcend mediocrity.
Sathya Sai Baba Speaks, Vol 5, p. 137*

Mediocrity haunts everything that diverts from itself. Why isn't it interested in opening its mind or widening its horizons and reaching knowledge? What is the reason that it is having such difficulties in realization? Michael Jackson knows that people don't know him and don't recognize him, not only the people who are indifferent in regard to him, but also the ones who call themselves his fans.

The whole world knows Michael Jackson, but there is nearly no one who knows him. Millions know Sathya Sai Baba, yet there is nobody who knows him. Are there two types of knowledge? What is knowledge? And what is realization? And what is necessary to reach knowledge and realization?

5. Knowing - Realization

What is the difference between knowing and realization? Do we know someone when we know his name? Do we realize someone when we have seen him?

Even today, the parable of the "tree of knowledge (realization)," from which Eve took the apple and gave it to Adam, is a mystery for man. Do we know what type of knowledge God is talking about when he speaks of the "knowledge of good and evil"?

Aldous Huxley is very clear about it, when he says that the goal of the human existence is to realize that "God is. That is the Ur-Fact. That we discover this fact by ourselves, by immediate experience, thus we are here for. The purpose and goal of every human is the realization which brings about unity that God is." *Huxley, 1996, p. 25**

Huxley claims that the realization that **God is** must

(1) be discovered by everyone by direct experience,

(2) this discovery is the purpose and goal of every human, and

(3) this realization brings about unity.

Why has man not yet progressed with this task? Why does he spend so much time looking for proof for God or proof that God does not exist?

Realization demands time, work and discipline and it is a process. Sathya Sai Baba describes the three phases of learning:

1. to absorb by reading or hearing,

2. to ponder on what is heard and to check it critically,

3. to contemplate on it meditatively.

...you cannot learn when you only hear something. You have to ponder on it and then conceive it intuitively.

Sathya Sai Baba, Summer Showers, Vol. 3, p. 107*

These three phases correspond to the three eyes of realization:

1. the eye of the flesh,

2. the eye of the mind and

3. the eye of contemplation, as Bonaventura states it.

People who think they know something after having heard or read about it didn't complete the process of learning, but are stuck in the first or second phase. How can anybody expect to look at things from a higher point of view when he only climbs the lowest steps of a ladder and stays there?

We are living in a time of consuming luxury goods, sensory pleasures and information. But as we do not process and digest the information, but only ingest it, the result is a disorder of digestion. Then it is easy to spit out the undigested so as to not get a stomachache. Our information society is acting exactly this way; it sullies others with undigested things and washes their hands of the matter in indignation.

Is it therefore surprising when knowing people don't throw pearls to swine? Many complain that Michael Jackson does not give many interviews and is afraid of the press. Studying his lyrics and rare interviews, we notice that the available material was not yet digested and processed. Who really has listened to Michael Jackson and understood his message? For what purpose are we asking for still more information? There is sufficient material for everyone who is really interested in knowledge and not in gossip. Also this book will not lift the veil of the mystery of Michael Jackson and Sathya Sai Baba, but only push it a little bit to the side.

What is happening in this example is nothing new. What is happening to the person Michael Jackson is true in a similar way for Sathya Sai Baba. In history of mankind all things that were not understood and what the limited mind cannot imagine - because it is lacking the power of imagination - were twisted in a way to fit into the limited imagination. People look for a drawer they would like to fill and thus the one in question can be disposed of. Thus the mental drawers are filled with "the funk of forty thousand years," as Michael calls it in his song Thriller, and there are only very few people who are interested in emptying these landfill sites. The habit of man to twist everything he doesn't like, to force it in the bed of Procrustes was already described in the Greek mythology. "Dogma turns man to an intellectual Procrustes. He attacks things and forces them to be signs of his word patterns whereas in reality he should adapt his word patterns so that we are signs of the things." *Huxley, 1996, p. 21**

Procrustes is a figure in the Greek mythology, a robber who put everyone who fell into his hands on a bed. If they were too short he stretched them and if they were to long he cut off a piece. Such schemes in which things are forced brutally dominate the mind of people. We are confronted with them on a daily basis and academic science is one of the busiest hirelings of the lobby of the devotees of the belief: "That which is not allowed cannot be." Scientists and even self-proclaimed realists suggest that these bulk products are the real thing.

Evolution demands that man widens his power of imagination, which he himself is narrowing and limiting. One who wants to reduce a greater power of imagination to a mediocre one gets stuck or regresses. The statement, "I cannot imagine this or that," is often used to avoid the expansion of the mind and hinders the realization or manifestation of creative ideas, because the first step to realization is the imagination in the mind, the creation of a mental image or a visualization. The power of imagination and the ability to think of something that does not exist in the physical world is not limited a priori but prevented by dogma. What reason should there be to only be able to imagine things that we have already seen with our physical eyes? The physical eyes have thus far only seen grey elephants, but why should one not imagine a pink or green elephant? I can imagine whatever I want. Only when I am open to the realms beyond the experiences of the five senses and allow ideas, thoughts and visions which expand my imagination, will the channel to the inner source of creativity open up, which is free from concepts and terms and is nourished directly from the source of wisdom. The method of brainstorming makes use of this creative potential, which belongs nowadays to the standard repertoire of all creative works and professions. Using this method, all ideas and imaginations which surge in relation to a certain question or problem are allowed and collected, without filtering them, without judgment, or to value its degree of reality. Measuring and weighing are features of the mind which hinder the flow of creativity. Progress starts with visions which are located in realms beyond mind.

An artist's imagination is his greatest tool. It can create a mood or feeling that people want to have, as well as transport you to a different place altogether.
Michael Jackson, Moonwalk, p. 159

Michael Jackson makes use of fantasy and creativity in an ingenious way in his works. The double album from 1995 is called "HIStory, Past, Present and Future, Book I." The way the word HIStory is written expresses in one word three possible meanings:

1. his story - the story of Michael Jackson
2. history - the story of mankind
3. His story - the story of the One, God.

Looking superficially the songs only deal with the person Michael Jackson; this was the opinion of most critics. Thereby they overlook that masters of their handiwork or artwork take themselves as an example to transmit something more profound and vaster. We are only to transmit things we have experienced ourselves in a way that can be recognized as authentic truth which we impart and share with those who want to partake in it. The more someone applies oneself, the closer will be the contact to the other until finally both touch each other and realize that they are one. What then will last is HIS story.

Ken Wilber describes "history...as a movement of human consciousness - as the story of the love affair between the human and the divine." *Wilber, 1997, p. 49**

HIStory past, present and future is that which was, is and will be. What changes with time is the form, but not the essence. Michael Jackson called his album "Book I." Does that mean that there will also be a "Book II"? Perhaps Michael Jackson wanted to express that there is only the Book I - One without a Second, advaita in Sanskrit, only the book of being. Such is at least the teaching of wise men and masters for ages.

An almost unknown work (in 1999) of Michael Jackson are his poems and thoughts "Dancing the Dream," which show his poetic and talent as a writer and express his profound understanding of life and creation and especially his limitless compassion for all living beings - of a quality we only find with Great realized Souls. He himself sees the 46 stories as more authentic than his biography "Moonwalk." They are an expression of a higher consciousness and a real treasure chest for every serious spiritual pilgrim.

Also the lyrics of his HIStory album "come from the heart; they are myself," says Michael Jackson. What does that mean - "myself"? The words "I, me, my" are the most used words and at the same time the words whose meaning is least understood and challenged. Who am I? What is the I? Who is myself? Sathya Sai Baba gives us a hint:

When you use the word "I" you have to consider that there are three types of "I." At one point it denotes the outer human form of the body; another "I" relates to the divine inside of the body. Between those two there is yet the "I" which expresses the life-giving part of the being.
Sathya Sai Baba, Summer Showers 4, p. 37*

Only ignorance uses the word "I" to indicate the body.
Sathya Sai Baba, Upanishad Vahini, p. 79*

When man is bound in the physical he is thinking of "his" money, "his" family, "his" property, "his" wife and "his" children and is strongly connected with them.
Sathya Sai Baba, Summer Showers 2, p. 161*

6.   Giving - Forgiving

Michael Jackson surrenders his work after completion to the world: "they are no longer my songs...they now belong to all"; he does not consider them as "his," but lets them go. He is not possessive towards them. What does he mean? Looking superficially one could think that he gives up his copyrights or the profits.

Looking more deeply, one can understand that he is not talking about the physical level, but the mental plane. One who understands that we are all only instruments fulfills his duty and gives his gift to humanity. Then humanity has to decide for itself what it will do with that gift. Everyone can deny it or accept it, use it or waste the opportunity. Michael Jackson gives his songs to the world to give and share with everyone what was given to him. "He is so giving of himself that, at times, he leaves very little to protect that beautiful inner core that is the essence of him," Elizabeth Taylor says about him. (Dancing the Dream, Introduction)
Michael Jackson writes:

I know my fate is to show others that this silence, this light, this blessing is my dance. I take this gift only to give it again. "Quick, give!" says the light. As never before I try to obey."
Michael Jackson, Dance of Life, Dancing the Dream

One who identifies with a narrow mind has the conviction that the result of giving is getting poorer and therefore tries to take as much as possible. This off-beam assumption is the reason for the restless search of man for fulfillment. Yet fulfillment can never be reached by taking but only by giving and sharing, as the dictum says: "Shared joy is double joy."

Sathya Sai Baba is asking from us:
Give, don't clutch to things with clenched fists. Let go, don't attach to others and don't let yourself be bound....There is no joy that equals the joy of sharing, giving and renouncing. You can understand this better when you pay attention to

40

the behavior of children. They are like realized souls, without bonds....A child has no yearning to possess others or to reject them. It does not collect for days to come or out of sheer pleasure to get famous one day as a collector. Maybe a child has a dirty body, but its mind is free from dirt. Older people are very accurate with their bodily cleanness, but their mind is a puddle of desires, hate, envy and dirty mud.
Sathya Sai Baba Speaks, Vol. 8, chap. 28*

Sathya Sai Baba always points in his speeches to the fact that we can learn from children. It is known that Michael Jackson had a special relationship with children for the same reason. He gives willingly as children do and he told us that this giving and sharing and the joy that comes from it makes him happy. "Genius is Childhood rediscovered," says Baudelaire, and Sathya Sai Baba calls to mind the purpose of humanness:

Everybody should consider the purpose of human life. The scriptures declare: "The body was given us to serve others." The body should not only be used for our own purpose, but for the well-being of others.
Sathya Sai Baba, Sanathana Sarathi, 10/1997*

"For me," "to me" - that is animal longing. "From me," "by me" - this giving is a sign of the divine nature of man. Divide, then the feeling of oneness is anchored, you lose all fear and discard all envy and will greatly grow in love.
Sathya Sai Baba Speaks, Vol. 8, chap. 28*

Man has to think again of service and love, that's the teaching of Sathya Sai Baba. Michael Jackson made this giving to his purpose in life, the giving of material help, but above the giving of joy. One of the new songs in 2000 is called, "What more can I give?" In the German show "Wetten Dass" on March 20, 1999 he confesses that this question was crossing his mind all the time and that he was inspired in a conversation with Nelson Mandela to give two charity concerts, one in Seoul and one in Munich.

We all have to give and we have to give everything we can to help and to end the unnecessary suffering in the world.
Michael Jackson, press release March 23, 1999, Sony Europe

The ability to forgive is strongly connected to the ability of giving.

The ego gets and forgets
  Love gives and forgives.
Sathya Sai Baba

The desire for revenge and vengeance was strange to Michael even in his young years. He always had difficulty understanding such a reaction by other people. He writes in "Moonwalk":

...I am fascinated by the concept of revenge. It's something I can't understand. The idea of making someone "pay" for something they have done to you is totally alien to me.
Michael Jackson, Moonwalk, p. 173f

Sathya Sai Baba sees this as a mark of people who are oriented materially.
The "normal" reaction of people is to pay like with like. Nevertheless this is a sign of the path which is directed outward, which deals with the material world.
Sathya Sai Baba, Sutra Vahini, p. 16*

Michael Jackson does not belong to this group, of normal people. He answers the question of talkmaster Oprah Winfrey of how he is dealing with his relationship with his father, who abused him very brutally as a child:

I love him. I forgive him.

Oprah Winfrey, who perhaps had expected the answer of a "normal" man, asks doubtingly again: "Can you really forgive?" and Michael confirms: "I forgive."

The ability to forgive belongs to the qualities of humans on higher levels of evolution; everyone who has suffered real or imagined injustice has probably experienced how much time it takes until one has overcome the wound and is able to forgive and to forget. Some people are not even able

42

to do this step until the last day of their earthly stay. Michael Jackson does not only embrace his physical family with forgiving but also people he never met personally.

I am ready to forgive the press or to forgive everyone. I was taught to love and to forgive; that's in my heart.
Michael Jackson, Oprah Winfrey show, 10th of Feb. 1993

What is the meaning of forgiving? Why do have people such a hard time with it? Working with patients I realized how they are clenching onto the intent to get someone to pay, when they feel treated unjustly. Then their mind is filled with revenge and vengeance and they do not feel able to proceed in life before the other one has paid for it.

These people are blind to their own reality and instead identified with their futile material body or petty emotions. In their ignorance they don't know that their desire for revenge and vengeance falls back on them - like a boomerang -, that it destroys them, that they are beaten up inside and weakened. Thereby they miss the chance to feel the huge freeing power that is inherited in forgiving, as Sathya Sai Baba clarifies:

The attitude of forgiving is the sign of a man ....
Sathya Sai Baba, Sanathana Sarathi, 1st of Jan. 1994*

Psychotherapist Chuck Spezzano introduces a 30-day program in his book, "To Be Happy is the Best Revenge" (Glücklichsein ist die beste Vergeltung), 1996), which helps the reader to learn the art of letting go.

People who are calling for revenge instead of forgiving are ignorant of the universal laws. Even Paul mentions this law clearly and simple in his letter to the Galatians: "For each one will bear his own load...whatever a man sows, this he will also reap" (Galatians 6:5,7)

This law states that all energy - be it in the form of thoughts, feelings, words or deeds - will in a cycle, like a boomerang - return to those who created and released it. In his letter to the Corinthians Paul states: "Now this I stated, he who sows sparingly will also reap sparingly and he who sows bountifully will also reap bountifully." (2 Corinthians 9:6)

Sathya Sai Baba reminds us in the same way 2000 years later:

Everybody can only eat the fruits of what he has sown. Only good deeds can bring good results. Your luck or suffering depends on the nature of your deeds.
Sathya Sai Baba, Sanathana Sarathi 11/1997*

7.   Metaphors and Parables

Michael Jackson's short films and his lyrics in songs and stories are complex and are so detailed and full of symbols that one can discover ever new things and there seems to be no point where one could say: "Now I have reached the core."

The exploration of the message starts with outwardness, with what is visible for the physical eye. After this starts the work to decode the message of the pictures and symbols, which is the more difficult part.

Michael Jackson's songs and films, especially since HIStory, tell us stories and histories in the three mentioned meanings: they deal with Michael Jackson's personal life history, with history of mankind and with the history of the Divine. Every work of art can be compared to an onion, where every layer is removed one after the other and with each layer we come nearer the core. Every reader, hearer and seer can decide by himself if he wants to look at the onion only from the outside or if he will peel one layer after the other. Only the one who struggles through all layers will reach the core, the essence of the message, and then he will realize surprisingly that he has reached his own Self.

Michael Jackson imparts his message in pictures, he speaks in parables and symbols as all the great masters of mankind and wise men are doing. What is the reason that Michael does not convey his message in a direct way? Let's listen to the answer in his poem "Two Birds":

It's hard to tell them what I feel for you. They haven't ever met you, and no one has your picture. So how can they ever understand your mystery? Let's give them a clue:

Two birds sit in a tree. One eats cherries while the other looks on. Two birds fly through the air. One's song drops like crystal from the sky while the other keeps silent. Two birds wheel in the sun. One catches the light on its silver feathers while the other spreads wings of invisibility.

It's easy to guess which bird I am, but they'll never find you.

Unless...

Unless they already know a love that never interferes, that watches from beyond, that breathes free in the invisible air. Sweet bird, my soul, your silence is so precious. How long will it be before the world hears your song in mine?

Oh, that is a day I hunger for.

Michael Jackson, Two Birds, Dancing the dream

What is the deeper meaning of this poem? Who are the two birds? Are you curious to know or are you satisfied to put these lyrics in the drawer labeled, "Read and Approved," or in another drawer? It is not quite harmless to get involved with knowledge. Faustus has already warned us:

Yes what is thus named recognition-1 Who is allowed to call the child with its true name? The few who recognized in this respect, who fondly did not save their heart replete, revealed their feelings, their seeing to the mob, were since ever crucified and burnt.

Goethe, Faustus, Night, 589-593

If you choose knowledge you have no choice than to follow the three-phase process of learning:

1. Absorbing
2. Pondering
3. Meditative contemplation

Most people stop after the first stage, and some few people ponder on the things read or heard. One who is really interested in the message of "Two Birds" will hold on at this point to take the time and read the poem again and again, read it with the heart, reflect the lyrics and ponder on it for a while. Only then will the true meaning open up, only by engrossing the mind in it and merging to the floor of the ocean. Pearls are not found at the beach, but only on the floor of the ocean, where one has to dive deep.

46

Lyrics full of meaning are mostly considered as beautiful after the first reading and then put into the drawer called "beautiful" like a wonderful sunset or rainbow. But at times those lyrics are not really understood and are put into the drawer called "I can't do anything with it." In both drawers they remain for many years until one day they are again discovered on the occasion of a house cleaning. One who wants to understand has to clear out the drawers of his brain warehouse. He can decide to start now and to do it now.

The one who hears the message recognizes the dilemma of humanity and has the opportunity of finding the way out the dilemma and to the solution. Who are the two birds? What mystery is surrounding the second bird? Why did nobody ever see his picture? Is there no picture available or are we not able to see it? What is love that does not interfere?

In the Gospel of Matthew we can read: "Therefore I speak to them in parables, because while seeing they do not see, and while hearing they do not hear, nor do they understand. In their case the prophecy of Isaiah is fulfilled, 'You will keep on hearing, but will not understand, you will keep on seeing, but will not perceive.'" *Matthew, 13:13,14*

The statements from different sources are all indicating the same direction. Even though man has eyes and ears, he does not see and not hear. Even though they have senses they don't catch the sense. How can the sense be figured out when we don't use our senses? Not the five senses nor the sixth or the seventh?

Only by seeing with the heart will we advance to the core, to the essence. By pondering which comes after using the senses, the sense will reveal itself, the nature, the being. With the five senses we catch the form, the texture, the taste, the smell and the sound. By pondering we transcend this and can reach the core, the essence, the being. Michael Jackson gives us a hint in this regard. He claims that the song of the second bird can be heard listening to his songs and regrets that nobody hears it. What is the reason? Michael Jackson thinks,

"They don't know the love that never interferes."

What is that, a love that does not interfere? In what does this love not interfere?

47

8.   Love that does not interfere

In the hymn, "Childhood," in the film "Free Willy 2" and on the HIStory album Michael asks:

Before you judge me, try hard to love me.

This is not only his personal wish, but the wish of all people in the world, who are suffering from the fact that they are only loved when they behave the way others want them to behave, everyone who is not loved because of himself, but because they adapt to the expectations of others and thereby deny themselves. They only get love after others have interfered in their life, when they have met certain conditions - conditional love.

We know expressions like "do it for my sake" or "if you loved me you would do this" or "everything I did was done out of love." This love is used to get something from others or to shape others due to one's expectations, putting them under pressure, or putting wrong things in the proper light, to influence the life of others, to exert force on others, in short: to interfere. The word love is used as an instrument for the purpose of manipulation. The word love is used more for fraudulent labeling than any other word on this planet. Peter Handke says: "For me there exists only caring as love or better: caring love, otherwise only infatuation." *Focus 88/1998**

Aldous Huxley says it more radically: "To love a creation more than we love God is idolatry. There are many forms to idolize, but all have one thing in common, that is selfish love." (Huxley, p. 28*) Michael Jackson trusted already in his early years a higher guidance, which showed him the right way:

God was at the top of my list of priorities. and my mother and father and brothers and sisters followed.

Michael Jackson, Moonwalk, p. 150

My mother...instilled in me a love of Him that I will always have.
Michael Jackson, Moonwalk, p. 12

"Baba has said that a big part of the love which humans express is lust in reality and not at all true love. Lust is an excessive longing for something or someone. It is longing enhanced to the extreme. Love means to let go and easy flowing, while lust is holding on and tight grasping." (Krystal, 1995, p. 7f*) Michael Jackson is aware of the danger of lust and he knows and talks about the way out:

I have to pray to God 'cause I know how lust can blind.
Michael Jackson, Dangerous

It's just in the devil's game of greed and lust.... Are you infected with the same disease of lust, gluttony and greed?
Michael Jackson, Money, HIStory album

One who wants to hold on and grasp tight has unavoidably to interfere and contravene the universal law of flowing, which says that nothing and nobody can be held onto, because all energy and everything alive is forever flowing, always moving. Holding on means death. True love is freedom and letting go.

The abuse of love is the strongest weapon of the ego, by which it tries to realize its selfish interests. The ego has given the name love to infatuation, attachment and dependency, and can thereby play its false game undetected, because its persiflage is the noble etiquette "love." The ego is always seeing and looking for its advantages; it lives and acts at someone else's expense. It sucks and abuses - for the simple reason that it is nothing by itself and is depending on the energy from others for its survival.

"Selfish love is clearly visible in the gross forms of sensual hedonism or in the striving for wealth, power and fame. Less obvious but not less fatal it appears in the exaggerated fondness for certain people, places, things or institutions." *Huxley, 1996, p. 29**

The most important sign of the ego is its tendency to separation, segregation and delineation. As there is no connection to the source of energy it has to tap energy from others. As those from which it is tapping energy consider themselves also as egos they are chasing energy too.

We can imagine the method of energy supply as follows: A network of people is trying to mutually chase energy one from the other. Everybody is filled after an successful energy chase and feeling good, while those from whom the energy was tapped feel empty, weak and sucked out. Therefore they start to chase energy themselves until they are filled and feel powerful and good.

Nearly all people are participating in this energy chasing game, all those who are living without knowledge about the real energy source and are therefore dependent on energy theft to survive. They pass highs and lows, ups and downs, are on top of the world or down in the dumps according to the result of their energy chase.

The sociologist James Redfield has described the mechanisms and reasons for the energy chasing in his pioneering perspective, "The Celestine Prophecies." "The fourth insight teaches that people are competing with each other for energy and that this fact has an influence on every encounter of people....The more we become aware of interpersonal dynamics, the more we realize that the energy we won by this procedure does not last for long." *Redfield/Adrienne, p. 105**

The competition for energy finds its expression in the endless search of people for love. When we thereby get at a point feeling that we have found love in another person we tend to hold on to her/him, even when she/he has already withdrawn from our grip. Thereby the one from whom we are seeking the love has like ourselves no access to the source of love, and what we can get at best is the energy that he won in the competition for energy and love from others.

So what is our fault in the search for love?

We are searching outward, with other people. Where do the others get it from? They also are seeking it with others, so that the search for love finally consists of an endless ramified net of people who are tapping each other due to the search of love. Humanity is endlessly competing for love. What would we think about a humanity that would compete all the time for a glass of water without having any clue of approaching the source of water? Michael Jackson indicates this error in "Love":

"Some people spend their lives looking for love outside themselves. They think they have to grasp it in order to have it."

Michael Jackson, Love, Dancing the Dream

In his Christmas speech, Sathya Sai Baba clarifies the terms:

Man of today is completely unaware of what is meant by the term love. Man equates longing to love. He believes that whatever he is yearning for originates from love. That is not true love. Love is totally free from longing. It is totally selfless. It does not expect something in return. It is all encompassing. It makes no difference between friend and foe.

By forgetting this universal selfless love and filling itself with selfish desires man has the fantasy to be filled with love. That is worldly attachment. It is far off love which flows from spirit inside. Spiritual love is limitless.

Sanathana Sarathi 01/1998*

An incident from 1993 in the ashram of Sathya Sai Baba clarifies what love that does not interfere is. A group of German, Italian and Malaysian devotees were sitting in front of Swami - that is the name his devotees are calling him lovingly - in the interview room. A rich man from Singapore, who had already gotten several watches as presents from Sathya Sai Baba, brought a watch as present for Swami. Sathya Sai Baba did not accept this present.

"Look," he said, *"this hand did never take anything."*

He extended the right hand with the palm downwards and said:

"This hand is always like this" and indicated thus that it always is giving. *"I am the one who gives,"* he added.

"But I only gave out of love," the devotee said. Sathya Sai Baba shook his head lovingly.

"Not out of love"! Always only "love, love, love," he said in English. After the third love was translated for the German group, he looked prankfully and said in German "Liebäh!"

(Note of the author: instead of "Liebe," the "Bäh" sounds like a sheep and is used in German to indicate a bad taste). *Sathya Sai Briefe, 65/1998**

That's it - when someone uses love to aim at something or to achieve something.

Sathya Sai Baba challenges us instead:
See good, hear good, do good - that is the way to God.

God is love. Western man believes in the contrary; he has chosen a punishing and loveless God and acts on this maxim. Accordingly he prefers to see bad things, hear bad things, do bad things. Many people are full of hatred, envy and outrage. That is the only explanation for the success of tabloids, yellow press and the ratings of television. Under the pretext of the obligation to inform we are offered trash, in which man can wallow. It is the nature of the human mind and the ego to be attracted by negativity, because they are necessary for their survival.

Sathya Sai Baba gave us the program for "Ceiling on Desires" to curb the self-indulgence of the mind and the ego. Man is also indulging in his desire to know, not true knowledge, but information. "Are you aware of how much trash we absorb nowadays?...How many of you read the magazines from beginning to the end, every sex scandal, every nonsense, which arises? We devour it. Do you know why? The magazines and media know that the human mind wants this type of negativity. They fill the magazines with this negativity and we devour it. Let's practice a spiritual exercise from now on. Are we able to ceil our desires while we see something about robbery, sex or murder in the magazines? Don't read that!" is the advice of scientist Jagadeesan (21st of Nov. 1998*)

Only the one who uses more than the five senses and whose heart is crying facing the actual state of the world can track the realization that Michael Jackson has in front of his image:

...the most I can do for the earth is to be its loving child. That one in the mirror winced and squirmed. He hadn't thought so much about love. Seeing 'problems' was much easier, because love means complete self-honesty. Ouch!

52

"Oh friend," I whispered to him, "do you think anything can solve problems without love?" That one in the mirror wasn't sure...."Is love more real than pain?" he asked.
Michael Jackson, Mirror, Dancing the Dream

Michael Jackson chose in his young years the more difficult way.
I was born to never die...to share my love without a sigh...
Michael Jackson, Ecstasy, Dancing the Dream

Because the song (the 2001 theme) was a celebration of love taking over, cleansing the sins of the world.
Michael Jackson, Moonwalk, p. 168

The biggest obstacle to progress is self-delusion whereby man tries to persuade himself that change has to start with others and oneself is unable to do something, because the other one does not want to cooperate. Michael Jackson writes:

Having fear is not the problem, because everyone feels anxious and insecure sometimes. The problem is not being honest enough to admit your fear....The deeper I go into myself, the stronger I become, because I realize that my real self is much bigger than any fear. In accepting yourself completely, trust becomes complete. There is no longer any separation between people, because there is no longer any separation inside. In the space where fear used to live, love is allowed to grow.
Michael Jackson, Trust, Dancing the Dream

When you have the courage to be intimate, you know who you are, and you're willing to let others see that....In spite of the risks the courage to be honest and intimate opens the way to self-discovery. It offers, what we all want, the promise of love.

Michael Jackson, Courage, Dancing the Dream

To open the way to love is the purpose of self-discovery and of the timeless challenge, "Know thyself!" When we are ready to embark on the journey to the heart we will realize that all creatures are escorting us and are here to support us on our journey, like the elephants do: So the elephants march on, and every tread beats out words in the dust: "Watch, learn, love. Watch, learn, love!" Can you hear them? One day in shame, the ghosts of ten thousand lords of the plains will say, "We do not hate you. Don't you see at last? We were willing to fall, so that you, dear small ones, will never fall again."

Michael Jackson, So the elephants march, Dancing the Dream

Even art and literature are filled with the "Song of Love," which reveals to everybody that there is no greater power than love, yet people try to solve the problems of their home planet with hate and attack. Examples from history which show that liberation is possible without force and attack - like the liberation of India or the fall of the Wall in Berlin - are not realized. Michael Jackson's words are as follows:

Silently, from one person to another, love kept up its invisible work. 'Stop it!' the Wall shrieked. 'I'm falling apart.' But it was too late. A million hearts had found each other. The Wall had fallen before it came down.

Michael Jackson, Berlin 1989, Dancing the Dream

"Love" deals with the omnipresence of love as a motivating power for everyone and everything:

When it's allowed to be free, love is what makes life alive, joyful, and new. It's the juice and energy that motivates my music, my dancing, everything. As long as love is in my heart, it's everywhere.
Michael Jackson, Love, Dancing the Dream

' Is love more real than pain?' he (the mirror) asked. 'I can't promise that it is. But it might be. Let's discover,' I said....'Let's not be alone again. Will you be my partner? I hear a dance starting up. Come.'
Michael Jackson, The one in the mirror, Dancing the Dream

Human behavior which is directed by love is a three-stage process. Most people climb up the first two steps, but only a minority reach the highest level. "The actions of love, that are produced by man, pass through three stages. The first is the connection between parent and child, the admiration and concern of the parents for the child and the affection and deification of the parents by the child, who chooses their example and model to deify them. The majority of the human race is living in this stage of evolution. Secondly, friendship, which exists in the exchange of consciousness, the joy of the connection and more or less loyalty and affection, due to the development of the life stream. Each one follows his individual path and allows only in times of crisis that the power of his love comes out. Third, the individuals who decide to put their love, their connection, their talents and their consciousness into ongoing service for the race (of humanity). Here we find a very small portion of people." *Book of Life, p. 172**

Michael Jackson uses every free hour for service for the benefit of man. He works in stillness. There is little known about his countless activities in the service of his fellowmen. i don't want to specify all his activities in this book, because that would fill another book. i only want to mention the trust, "Heal the World," founded in 1992, and the trust, "Make a Wish." The purpose of the first one is to support distressed children all over the world, and the second wants to fulfill the last wish of dying children who want to meet Michael Jackson. Michael Jackson invites children to his

Neverland Ranch several times a month, where they pass the whole day together and the shining in the eyes of the children makes Michael happy beyond description and encourage him to continue these activities.

Anyone who wants to know the details and see the facts will find them on various websites, for instance www.mjfc-jam.com or www.mjfriendship.de or in the "Black & White Magazine on mjjshop.com. But know - you will find facts there - not gossip.

Few people know that Michael Jackson was nominated twice for the Nobel Peace Prize, in 1995 and 1998.

The three stages of the evolution of the power of love correspond to the evolution of man from the animalistic to the human to the divine level. The stage of the parent-child connection we can already find with animals and is directed mostly by instinctive behavior. An example is the cuteness of small children, which means that the physiognomy and the chubby and cute expression on the face of babies and small children evokes the protective and caring instinct in man and animals. Highly evolved souls indeed are no longer directed by instincts, but by their consciousness. This is possible when old programmed patterns are resolved, as for example the destructive emotions, which Sathya Sai Baba titles as the six enemies of mankind: anger, hate, jealousy, pride, delusion and greed.

Michael Jackson experienced this destructive force first hand in 1992 and 1993, when he became the victim of an evil campaign of slander. The world press at the time exploited the issue and duplicated the dirt for months. Even though in the meantime the facts about this collusive game were well known, which Mary A. Fischer calls in her detailed report "a story of greed and envy," until now nobody was really interested in the rehabilitation of Michael Jackson ("Was Michael Jackson Framed?", GQ Magazine, October 1994; and also as book, October 4, 2012). With this information not much money can be earned.

The ramping and raging demonic qualities have to be overcome and transformed, when man wants to progress from the animalistic to the human stage to finally arrive at the divine level. Sathya Sai Baba tells us:

There are three types of human behavior: the divine, the human and the animalistic. We can witness how the animalistic is growing and the human behavior is degenerating. The reason for this trend is the unlimited growing of desires and the permanent disappearing of ideals. Selfishness is growing, selflessness is lessening. Cheating is widening, integrity is disappearing.
Sanathana Sarathi, 11/1997*

Some people hear the message and follow the call of their soul. They transcend the stages of the egocentric and sociocentric world view and reach the worldcentric view. They are not only interested in their own welfare and that of their immediate environment, but filled with love for all living beings, independent of their level of evolution, and they are filled with an authentic wish and spurred by an unrestrained longing to serve the entirety of humanity and the welfare of the planet. They have understood that all kingdoms - starting with the mineral kingdom, the plant and animal kingdom to the human kingdom - are interwoven and that the chain of being or better the network of being (Wilber 1999) is reaching beyond humanness to the kingdom of the angels and gods - to the kingdom of pure being or the Absolute. Oprah Winfrey asked Michael what he was feeling standing on stage in front of a ocean of people.

Love...
Oprah Winfrey Show, 11th of Feb. 1993

Try to develop divine love. Love is God, Life is God. The best way to love God is loving everything, serving everyone. All are embodiments of God.
Sathya Sai Baba, Sanathana Sarathi, 02/1998*

There is a duty that is common to all stages of life, that is the duty which is dictated by the heart. Fill your heart with love. Thus you can reach everything. Begin the day with love. Fill the day with love. End the day with love. That is the way to God.
Sanathana Sarathi, 02/1998*

Michael Jackson repeats his message unwaveringly despite all the trials to ridicule him. "I love you, I love you, I love you." And when people respond with "We love you," he ups the ante with "I love you more." This he not only declares in his mother tongue, but in all languages of the countries he is visiting - more than forty in five continents. How many of his listeners did not even hear this sentence once? The one who thinks these words to be a brilliant publicity gag should deal with chapter 34, "The wisdom of the mirror".

9.   Fan

Michael Jackson thinks love to be the motivating power even for behavior that is not understood immediately. Instead of judging and condemning those who are making his life a hell, his well-marked empathy is allowing him to have deep insight beyond the outward and recognizes the behavior as a manifestation of love. For this "deep insight," the eye of contemplation is needed so that the eye can be directed to the purpose instead of to the instrument. Thus unholy instruments will lose their destructive force.

"Being mobbed by near hysterical girls was one of the most terrifying experiences for me in those days. I mean it was rough. We'd decide to run into some department store to see what they had, and the fans would find out we were there and would demolish the place, just tear it up....When those mob scenes broke out, all the craziness and adulation and notoriety became more than we could handle. If you haven't witnessed a scene like that, you can't imagine what it's like. Those girls were serious. They still are. They don't realize they might hurt you because they're acting out of love. They mean well, but I can testify that it hurts to be mobbed. You feel as if you're going to suffocate or be dismembered....I know the fans mean well and I love them for their enthusiasm and support, but crowd scenes are scary."

Michael Jackson, Moonwalk, p. 90f

People who are permanently in the spotlight or - as Michael Jackson calls it - living in an aquarium, are confronted with an enormous subtle pressure and are robbed their energy. Only a few celebrities are able to tolerate this energy vampirism. Legion are those who were broken by this pressure and sought refuge in drugs, alcohol and sex.

What enables someone to look at the purpose instead of the behavior? Where does the power come from to love those who cause us suffering? What are the qualities of a love that is giving and sharing generously?

It is the inevitable result of human evolution, when it reaches the subtle levels of being, where people can see the unmanifested with the eye of contemplation. Michael Jackson's lyrics show that he was seeing with this eye of the heart. When we advance into the depth of our inner world, then the color of the glasses we are using to see the outer world changes automatically. With the eye of contemplation we reach the place "which is love," and learn to see with the glasses of love.

"Fans" claim to love their idols. This veils the destructive character of their fanaticism. Fans are chasing energy, want to bogart their idols and suck them. They are on the egocentric level of evolution and are not capable of empathizing with those whom they are adoring. They put their idols on a pedestal to admire and idolize them as false gods and suck them like vampires. They are dancing "around the golden calf." It provides for them a projection surface, whereon they project everything which they, due to their wrong sight, cannot find in themselves and instead are searching for it in others. "Fan" means also blower, and thus they are behaving like beings that are wildly twisting around their axes, who disperse whole energy centrifugally outwards. By this orientation to the outward they develop a feeling of inner emptiness, that they try to fill by bogarting the idol. It would be a better service to the world and all human beings in the state of role models when their admirers and adorers would behave like friends - instead like fans. Michael Jackson calls his charity concerts on 25th and 27the of June 1999 "Michael Jackson & Friends." This relates not only to his friends with whom he was performing, but also to all those who follow his ideals instead of him as idol. These friends don't need to chase energy, but help themselves from the source of the ideal, whose reservoir is inexhaustible. Every time we take from takers the reservoir is restricted to that which was taken by the taker. When we on the other hand are givers, everything is available. James Redfield writes in his "Handbook to work with the nine Insights"???: "Step by step we come to realize that the true energy is coming from an universal source. There is no necessity to provide energy through other persons." (Redfield p. 106*). His book is studded with concrete exercises and orientations which help us to tap the source instead of other people.

What is hindering people to search for the source of energy? They look at life as an end in itself with the only purpose to have fun and to make one's life pleasant. They are not allowed to stop on the chase for sensual pleasures and amusement to not feel the emptiness which is left behind these superficial enjoyments. To fill the emptiness they jump like greedy vultures on everything with promises to fill this emptiness - if only for one short moment.

Creatures crawl in search of blood.
Michael Jackson, Thriller

You got blood lust for me.
Michael Jackson, 2 Bad

Here are active the six enemies of man or - as is said in the Gospels - the "beast" (*Revelation 13:18*). The beast is lusting for the blood, the life energy, of other people to nurture itself. Biology calls them parasites, mythology vampires.

"My task is the research on violence between people. We always knew that behind this violence we can find the desire to control and reign over other people....We don't try to control or trick each other to reach a certain goal, but because we achieve an energy thrust controlling others. That is the reason for the existence of many seemingly irrational problems in the world - on individual as well as national level." *Redfield, 1994, p. 93/94**

These control patterns are forwarded from generation to generation, when we don't realize the psychodynamics behind them and solve the problem by pulling out the roots. We have shown the way out - instead of sucking others we have to tap the energy source in our own inner selves.

Only this way will the dignity of all people in the world be restored instead of degrading them to objects of greed.

The example of Michael Jackson shows how much suffering is caused by this chasing of energy. He spoke about the high price of his high profile. For 36 years (in 1999) - nearly a whole working life - he is chased at every turn, is continuously stared at by millions and millions eyes.

I spent my whole life living in an aquarium and I want my son to live a normal life.

Michael Jackson , OK magazine, 4th of April 1997

Instead of using the great achievements of modern media technology like internet, television, and radio to improve the quality of life of all humans, man abuses them to disturb himself from the purpose and goal of being human. An instrument, tool or means is not good or bad by itself, but it is used or abused. A knife in the hands of a surgeon is used for the benefit of man, while in the hands of a murderer it is abuse. If we want to prevent abuse, the user has to change, not the instrument.

Michael Jackson is pleading in favor of using the possibilities of the mass media to solve the problems of the world and humanity.

I believe passionately in the power of mass entertainment and have seen how - with positive messages - it can help alleviate the problems we face, including the suffering of the world's children

Michael Jackson, spring 1993, formerly: www.mjifc.com, now: www.michaeljackson.ru

Oprah Winfrey also testifies at times, "I love television," when she succeeded in contributing with a show that is moving people and touches their soul, so that they head on the path to their true home. Regularly she is contributing with shows that deal with the issue, "To bethink in Spirit," where wisdom has its say.

The time has come to create a balance between giving and taking. We have to re-member that we all are embodiments of God and to link to the source inside, fill us and thus find fulfillment. Then we have no more need to use others as energy suppliers, but will follow the principle of unity of giving and taking.

The one who is linked to himself does not interfere, but is waiting in stillness until the veil will also lift for the rest of mankind. He then follows Jesus' command and prayer: "Forgive them for they know not what they do." (*Luke 23:34*)

The image of the world as an energy pattern gives the lie to our accustomed image of the world as a heap of material. The scientist Stephen Wolinsky provided us with a brilliant synthesis of science and ancient wisdom under the term of "quantum psychology." The consequences which follow turn our former image of the world upside down.

They say that everything we believed to be true until now is untrue and that everything we believed to be untrue is true. The quintessence of scientific discoveries of the last decades is in accordance with what the mystics of all times and of all cultures always were claiming, that the basis of the universe is pure consciousness - or energy in modern terminology - and that nothing does exist besides this One. The search for an objective measurable world is an illusion. The fetish of science - the objectivity - has to be buried.

The mechanistic world image of Newton, Descartes, Darwin and Freud, which took up under the pretext of the Age of Enlightenment, which means to bring light into the darkness, turns out to be in the light of realization of reality as idealization and superstition. The physical eye is not capable of seeing the vibrating energy pattern effected by light. That can only be grasped with the eye of contemplation, the inner eye, and can then enlighten the mind and - our sight will finally be clear.

There is nothing in the universe besides this spiritual light. The border which we see with the physical between bodies, things and forms does not exist on the base level. They are an illusion of the senses and the result of the collective trance, which is the state of humanity.

The consciousness of the masses is always the mediocrity. In statistics we know the "normal distribution" of characteristics as discovered by

Gauss. It says that 68 percent of the characteristics of a population deviate 10 percent from the empirically determined average value. Most characteristics adhere to this normal distribution, which means that two-thirds of the population have characteristics around the average, that means they are average or normal.

Less than one-sixth of the population has characteristics which deviate more than ten percent above or below the average value.

When we ask someone if he thinks himself to be normal, he will probably answer "yes." But when we ask the same person if he thinks himself to be mediocre, he will surely say "no." He has answered the same question once with yes and once with no. The reason for this answering is the trance in which he is staying together with the rest of mankind. To resolve this trance man has to set his sights on the purpose and know himself instead of identifying with countless labels.

Only by birth as human being can God be realized. To waste time is the biggest foolishness....Here and now we are given the opportunity to realize the last absolute goal.
Sathya Sai Baba, cit. in Hislop, p. 149*

People who do not adapt to this "normal" image are skeptically fancied and often marked down as outsiders. This is paradox because mediocrity tends to orient itself outwards, that means is an outsider, while those who orient themselves inwards, should be called insiders or better - insighters.

Whether you see something as outside or inside depends on your standpoint. By the standpoint is created the direction, whereby all who are standing on the same side as the observer are looked at as insiders and all people on the other side as outsiders. But in the moment you change your standpoint or turn the coin this assessment is no longer valid. Objectivity does not exist. Objectivity is an illusion, as has been taught by the Vedanta for centuries and milleniums.

10.   From animal to human

Consciousness researcher Ken Wilber has shown that humanity is actually at "half time of evolution" on the way from animal to the Divine. Many people equal a carriage driver who has handed over the reins and let their horses gallop wherever they want. These horses are the wishes and desires which behave like animals. To reach his goal man has to overcome his animalistic nature, to tame it and to rein it. Only then he can lead his carriage to the Divine.

Michael Jackson paints a film image of how our society is dealing with the "non-normal" in his film, "Ghosts." This society persecutes the non-normality of humanness out of shabby pretenses under the banner of the normality of the animalistic.

Normal people, who live a normal life, with normal children and normal adults, are living in Normal Valley and follow their normal mayor to quite normally chase the "Maestro" - the Master - out of the palace, because he is not normal and represents a threat to the normal. The danger that the children are contaminated by the non-normal has to be banned. Everything that cannot be grasped and caught (mentally) has to be grasped and caught (physically), because normality cannot tolerate what is not understood. What is not mediocre, not measurable, not weighable, not gaugeable, what does not fit in the bed of Procrustes has to be forced in or cut back. It is persecuted, removed and deported.

The film "Ghosts" shows strongly where the ghost of jealousy and greed is leading, who normality is seeking eagerly for that which it can destroy, attack and hate. By threatening the master with violence he shall be deported. It is obvious that the children are not as normal as they should be, as they are fascinated and enthusiastic about the "master," are feeling his attractive power and express their joy, when their eyes meet. The normal citizens try to prevent the attractive power of the Maestro by direct and indirect threats. While the children find life, joy, excitement and enthusiasm with the Maestro, the normal adults are following their mayor. While the Maestro is master of life, the mayor is master of the citizens. A master is one who masters something or others. While the master of life masters life, the master of the citizens masters the citizen. While the children impatiently react to the love and joy of the master of life, the adults are blinded by the hate and envy of the master of the citizens.

While the children feel the humanness and the connection from heart to heart, the adults are torn inside and don't have the courage to follow their hearts. They are inhibited by the suggestive power of their mayor, who is green with envy.

Tell me are you the ghost of jealousy?
Michael Jackson, film "Ghosts" and "Blood on the Dance floor"

At the end the mayor turns insane and destroys himself, mad and blinded by rage, in his persecution mania of everything that lies beyond normality, beyond mediocrity. The law of balancing is fulfilled - we have to reap what we have sown. He who destroys others destroys himself.

Egoism is accompanied by a horrible disease named greed. There are possibilities for healing for all sort of diseases in the world. But there is no remedy for egotism as well as envy and hate. The only healing for these two diseases is complete ruin.
Sathya Sai Baba, Sanathana Sarathi, 11/1997*

Jealousy is a disease with no cure.
Sathya Sai Baba, Sanathana Sarathi, 12/1998*

The citizens are finally able to open up for the dimension of life, after they are rid of their mayor. Their faces lighten up, they are again able to laugh and tune in hesitatingly to the "game of life."

Peter Handke describes this miserable state of humanity as follows: "Previously, as children, they sought for the sight to open up themselves. Now their sight only is serving to compete with others....Writing is rediscovering of childhood by deciphering, that is of childlike marveling and looking forward." *(Focus 8/1998*)*

We are closed off from the real "Game of Life" due to our attachments and dislikes. Sathya Sai Baba says it drastically:

The mind is filled by these twofold feelings (attachment and aversion). Thus he tends to forget his basically human nature. The mind considers in this state the basic six enemies of man - lust, hate, delusion, greed, envy and pride - as virtues. These six vices can poison the entire being of someone. He then forgets his inherent divinity and ceases to be human.
Sathya Sai Baba, Sanathana Sarathi, 11/1997*

But I think music soothes the savage beast. If you put cells under a microscope and you put music on, you'll see them move and start to dance. It affects the soul.
Michael Jackson, Ebony, May 1992

11. Man - Hu-man

Man is truly divine, an image of God. "Is it not written in your law, I've said you are gods?" (*John 10:34*), says Jesus to the Jews and thus is the teaching of all Holy Scriptures, the Bible, the Veda, The Upanishads, the Bhagavadgita, the Tao Te Ching, the Quran, etc. But up until today man has been living as a travesty of himself. The word "man" is derived from the Sanskrit term "manu." It does not describe the gender, but the race of humanity. In German "man" also means "one" and militant feminists replaced it with the term "woman" in the misguided assumption to reach thereby equal rights for both genders. If we would follow the spirit of the law instead of the letter, we would not fall in the trap so often. "Manu" is the progenitor, the primal father of mankind; he is the epitome of man. This is not of male gender, but androgynous, genderless. Michael Jackson is often labeled androgynous. As we use language to communicate with each other we are forced to determine a gender. But we should be careful not to reduce the language of the spirit to the language of the body.

Man actually uses only a small portion of his potential; he is still in the embryonic state of evolution and still has to unfold his very own essence. Unfold, un-fold means that it is already present in a folded form, but has like a bud not yet come to full blossom. The fully blossomed man is divine, but first he has to express his humanness. When we say of someone, "He is so human," we are referring to qualities we do not find within all humans. We therefore experience humanness as something special, something we consider to be worthy of extra mention. Humanness is a characteristic we don't find in everyone who is wandering in the body of a human. To say about a human that he is so human, is the same as saying about sugar, it is sweet. Normally the sweetness of sugar does not need to be mentioned because it is the sweetness that defines sugar. Sweetness is the very essence of sugar, its Dharma as called in Sanskrit. Notsweet sugar is a paradox in itself. Nothuman humans are also a paradox in themselves and yet they exist. How long will it take until man lives his essence, his nature, realizes his Dharma? Until he becomes really human?

Michael Jackson introduced on 20th of March 1999 in the German show "Wetten Dass" his project "Adventure Humanity," as it was called by Dr. Peter Walker from the International Red Cross. In cooperation with the Red Cross, UNESCO and the Nelson Mandela Trust, he gave two charity concerts together with more than sixty artists from the United States of America, Germany, Italy, Korea, France, England, Ireland, Russia, Israel, Austria, India etc. These concerts took place in Munich and Seoul. Germany was chosen as a place for the event, because it had been reunited ten years before, and this would express symbolically the same vision for North and South Korea, playing the second concert in Seoul.

When the whole of humanity embarks on its "Adventure Humanity," we will have brought "Heaven to Earth" and can then wander in the "Garden of Eden."

12. Death of the object

Every observer influences everything he is observing. The observed is not something stable, substantial, objective, but the observed changes depending of the observer. "The most important cognition of quantum physics for the human experiencing and behavior says: 'The observer influences the reality created by him' (Heisenberg) and 'reality is created by observation.' Without observation the reality not exists." Copenhagen Interpretation, part II (*Wolinsky, 1993, p. 280**)

The fact that observation creates reality is called the "Heisenberg indeterminate principle." It says that there is no objective reality, but that which everyone considers as reality is the product of his own consciousness and thus subjective. It means that the observer during observation is judging and evaluating and is in reality observing, judging and evaluating himself; that means he evaluates the reality which was created by him. Critics don't critique the product of others, but they project their consciousness on the product and mirror in their critique and their judgment themselves. The critic is the creation of the criticizing person and uses the object of his critique only as a reflective surface for their own consciousness. "If you interact with another person, delusion is a part of the dynamics. This delusion allows every soul to perceive what it should understand to heal. It creates like a living film the situations that are necessary to bring the aspects of each soul which need healing into wholeness. (*Zukav, 1990, p. 206**)

Everything we accept or reject in others mirrors what we accept or reject within ourselves. The separation of the world into good and bad, holy men and sinners, in right and wrong, has nothing to do with the world in itself, but is a mirage due to the trance in which the observer is standing and which he is projecting outward. The picture which is perceived in the outside has the same degree of reality as a Fata Morgana. It is a mirage, or hot air.

Sight directed outwards is not able to discriminate, but only to judge. Judgment indeed divides the primal, the original, while only inward sight can reveal reality, can give insight, in-sight. (In German judgment is Urteil, which is composed of "primal" (Ur) and "part" (Teil).)

To separate the wheat from the chaff means to discriminate the shell from the core. This is only possible when the eye looks through the forms, when one sees the spirit instead of the letter. Michael Jackson's film "Teaser" (*HIStory on film, Vol. II*) can serve as a test for these two types of seeing. One who sees this film with the outer eyes instead with inner, the eye of the heart, will miss its quintessence.

They fell into my trap, says Michael Jackson about those who compared "Teaser" with Leni Riefenstahl's "Triumph of Will." The title "Teaser," which also means jester, or to belabor someone, already alerts us to be careful. We also know from the ancient teachings that the Avatar Krishna loved to tease the milkmaids in the village where he grew up as a little boy. "Teaser" was vehemently combated and disparaged by those who only looked at it with the eyes of the flesh. With analyses that are built on the eye of contemplation it is not possible to earn a lot of money. For scandal stories written out of rapacity they "even sell my soul to the devil" *(Michael Jackson, Money)*.

Albert Gaulden writes: "To all this whole mess a joking God added even money to see how much the grubby urchins would twist themselves to earn or save a dollar. They only need to assist television or open the magazines to see how many people are ready to kill for some cents or to give up their whole liberty for the big money. Behind this whole desire for money, property and prestige we find a low sense of self." *(Gaulden, 1007, p. 187*)*

We can realize how twisted our society is and how we abuse "liberty" when we are so free to make innocent people into prisoners and take from them their freedom to move freely. The following description about the life of Lady Diana Spencer could also be written in a biography of Michael Jackson when we replace the word "palace" with "society." "Diana the difficult one, was a problem, the palace could not deal with, but Diana the holy one, is a problem which the palace will never be able to handle. ... She showed real goodness, which is threatening for those at the other end of the spectrum of morality. ... Her language was not that of words. ...

The media would yet never have understood and valued her, because Diana was not of their world and did not share their values. When she looked at a rose she enjoyed its beauty, but those counted the petals." (*Morton, 1997, p. 252f**)

I'm the knower and the known ... the creator and creation merge into one wholeness of joy.
Michael Jackson, The Dance, Dancing the Dream

"The knower and the known turn into One. ... We can turn into the known as well as the knower, when we complete the two and bring them together. The problem is that we make a separation, where in reality is none." (*Spalding, Vol. 4, p. 77**)

We divide the One into two and play the game of duality by determining one half as giver and the other half as receiver, one as the observer and the other as the observed, one as object and the other as subject....The realization that you are not two but one, will fill you with consciousness and bliss.
Sathya Sai Baba Speaks, Vol. 8, p. 55*

13. Un-labelling

The realization that everything which exists is energy opens us up to the possibility of resolving energy blockages and releasing the blocked energy, that let float freely. The labels we have put on things and living beings have to be removed to perceive their essence, to see the truth of the being. Again the questions which lead us to realization are: "Who am I? Where do I come from? Where do I go?"

Let's take the example of a rose. What is a rose? The only thing we can certainly say about a rose is: "A rose is a rose is a rose is a rose is a rose...." That's all and that is sufficient. Everything we add, all characteristics and features, reduce the rose to something that is less than the quality "rose." With every addition concepts are created which block energy, which is then not available because it was used to construct the concept. I'm not saying that biologists and chemists should not do research about the rose scientifically. What I want to say is that we can only discover, dis-cover, the essence of the rose, that which makes a rose a rose, if we desist of analyses, measurement and concepts and concentrate directly on the realization of the rose, that is, if we look at it with the eye of the heart or the eye of contemplation.

Real art is universal and not limited to societies and cultures. Its deeper purpose is to overcome and transcend the supposed differences and separation, between East and West, between Head and Heart, between Spirit and Body, between Matter and Energy, between Man and God. To fulfill this purpose stuck patterns and solidified meanings are resolved, so that the blocked energy can be freed and disposable. Real freedom uses free-floating energy for a certain purpose and releases it again into the energy reservoir after having fulfilled this purpose. Metaphorically speaking: We fill the balloon with air only for as long as we want it to fly; after that we release the air again. If we don't release the energy of life after having used it, than the whole universe will consist only of full balloons and there will be no air left to breathe.

73

Exactly that is the case in relation to patterns of feeling and thinking. The reason that we are feeling unfree is that we in the most real sense of the word are moving through an invisible universe whose energy is filled with balloons, i.e., blocked in patterns of feeling and thinking.

The reactions of critics and the public to Michael Jackson's films "Teaser" and "Black or White" (*HIStory on film, Vol. II*) illustrate these blockages. Scarcely anybody takes special trouble to decode the message, because he enters his trance through certain sign stimulus and balloons of judgment block his view. In the case of art it is decisive to find out the message the artist wants to transmit and not slapdash impose one's own projections on his artwork.
Michael Jackson tells us about "Teaser" in an interview with Diane Sawyer:

I wanted everybody's attention....Symbol has nothing to do with that. It's not political, it's not fascist, it's not dogma. It's not ideology and all this stuff. It's pure, simple love. You don't see any tanks. You don't see any cannons. It's about love. It's people coming together....It's art. It's art.
Michael Jackson , Diane Sawyer Show, 14th June 1995

Certain patterns to feel and to think are so bred-in-the-bone that we are able to release them only for a short time. In "A Course in Miracles" it is said: "Simplicity is very difficult for a twisted mind" (T 14, II, 2,3*).

Symbols are signs whose meanings are not directly available to everyday consciousness, but which have an effect on a more subconscious level. They are signs that have been filled with energy for a long time by mental images and imaginations and are accordingly forceful and powerful. In the course of history, symbols have now and again been abused, such as the Swastika, the Christian cross, etc. It is possible to dissipate this abuse and to free the negatively qualified energy.

When we want to release a symbol which is filled with hate energy, we have to assail this symbol for a long time with the mental power of love, until step by step the hate energy drips out and is replaced completely by love energy.

The symbol of the cross was associated by Christianity with suffering and being able to bear, so that it is accompanied by a certain heaviness. In its deeper meaning it is yet a symbol for the saving of man, whereby the vertical beam signifies the ego and the horizontal one the erasing, the crucifixion of the one.

Cut the "I" feeling clean across and let your ego die on the Cross, to endow you with Eternity.
Sathya Sai Baba, cit. in Fanibunda, 1976, p. 0

Michael Jackson used as the logo for his venture, "Kingdom Entertainment," the symbol of the sword that we know from the saga of the Holy Grail. This sword Excalibur which is stuck in a rock can according to the saga only be pulled out of the rock by the most noble and most pure knight. In the song HIStory Michael sings:

Every hero dreams of chivalry
Every soldier dies in his glory
Every legend tells of conquest and liberty.
Michael Jackson, HIStoy

The saga of the Grail tells us in a coded way which sort of conquest and liberty we are dealing with, that of the ego, that of the delusion of a separated i, with which we are wrongly identified. This delusion is like a Fata Morgana which mirrors for us a reality that does not really exist. Liberty is the recognition of our immortality and Divinity, when the ego is cut clean across.

Experiences of all kinds, whether they be comfortable or uncomfortable, lead to the formation of feeling and thinking patterns and establish themselves within us as in a film, so that every time we experience something that is similar to a picture in this film, the whole film is automatically reeled and the pattern from the past activated. We then don't react in a proper manner to the new situation, but repeat

75

unconsciously the old pattern. Stephen Wolinsky researched this phenomenon and ascertained that it has to do with trance phenomenon. People live in a sort of hypnosis and are no longer able to realize reality. Furthermore they have no control over their feelings and thoughts. These deep trances hinder us from living in the present; instead an incident from the past takes place which is projected on the present. Trance states are not, as most assume, exceptional states but everyday phenomena with the majority of people, which distort the perception, the feelings and the thoughts. People without states of trance are very rare, because intensive self-exploration, willingness to be sincere to oneself and disciplined work are required to recognize and release these patterns that have been programmed by our own experience, by society, by education and schooling. "To hurt basic unity means to isolate oneself in a hypnotic estate, where you seem to be a separated being." (Spalding, Vol. 4, p. 185*)

Only when we stay in the present and remain there do we reach the essence. Only then do we see everything as it is. IT IS – ONE.

When we look at the world with pink glasses we will see a pink world and when we use grey glasses we will see a grey world. People with grey glasses do not understand that their world is as dreary as it is due to their grey glasses - and not because the world itself is grey.

You are wearing colored glasses and are seeing everything through these glasses. Correct this sight, and then the world will be corrected. Reform yourself, and then the world will be reformed.
*Sathya Sai Baba, Sanathana Sarathi, 08/1997**

Sathya Sai Baba encourages us to not pay attention to "small minds":
Those who are devoted to God should try to cleanse and to sanctify the atmosphere by developing love and practicing human values. It is possible that they have to face opposition and discouragement from some corners. They should overcome these obstacles. These critics are like pests which destroy extremely valuable things. Those who are engaged in charity should not care about these critics, but continue with their work according to the dictum of their conscience. ... If you are persuaded that what you are doing is good for people, why then should you care about the criticism of small minds? Develop self confidence!
*Sathya Sai Baba, Sanathana Sarathi, 11/1997**

Keep the faith...just keep...your feet flat on the ground...
I know that keepin' the faith means never giving up on love
But the power that love has to make it right, makes it, makes it right.
Michael Jackson, Keep the Faith

When we look at the world with love we will see love, and when we look at the world with hate we will see hate. The assumption that our neighbor is wearing the same glasses as we and has to have the same opinion as we is naive and delusional. Unfortunately most people wear grey glasses most of the time and are thus able to encourage each other most of the time in their dreary sight. We can observe this at every cracker-barrel and every coffee klatch. When others have the same opinion as we do, it is only proof that they are seeing the same. It says nothing about reality itself, but only about the color of the glasses.

Truth will not turn into untruth because it is not recognized. People have a hard time understanding those with other-colored glasses than their own. That is the reason for the existence of parties, organizations, associations, clubs, societies, unions, groups and every sort of coalition, where people meet who are wearing the same glasses. These groups are not aware that their coalition and their feeling of belonging as well as their actions and activities are the result of their identical glasses and hinder the interest and the access to truth and reality.

Jesus showed us the exit to all this by challenging us to follow him. He was talking literally, not only symbolically, when he said: "Truly truly I say to you, he who believes in Me, the works that I do, he will do also, and greater works than these he will do." (*John14:12*) "I am the living bread that came down from heaven. Whoever eats this bread will live forever." (*John 6:51*)

Sathya Sai Baba confirms the urgency of following Jesus for every Christian in his Christmas Speech in 1979:

You are only true Christians when you follow his (Jesus) teachings and apply them in your daily life. It would be sufficient if you follow only two of his teachings. Christ said to John: "All life is One, my son, therefore love everyone." If

you would follow this advice you could reach your destination. When he hung on the cross in agony he heard a voice from heaven saying: "Death is the dress of life." The body is the dress which the Divine puts on....The language of love is spoken and understood by all hearts. In reality there is only one race, and that is the race of humanity. That is the message Jesus brought us.
Sathya Sai Baba Speaks, Vol. 11, p. 18f*

14.   The Race of Humanity

Michael Jackson was feeling the longing to unite humanity since childhood. As the means to this goal, he saw his talent, the music and the dance.

Our first world tour had focused our interest in uniting people of all races through music....Music is color-blind....It's been my dream since I was a child to somehow unite people of the world through love and music.

Michael Jackson, Moonwalk, p. 147, p. 252

I wanted to do an album that was like Tchaikovsky's Nutcracker Suite. So that in a thousand years from now, people would still be listening to it. Something that would live forever. I would like to see children and teenagers and parents and all races all over the world, hundreds and hundreds of years from now, still pulling out songs from that album and dissecting it. I want it to live.

Michael Jackson, Ebony, May 1992

It don't matter if you're black or white...
And I told about equality and it's true...
It's not about races, just places, faces
Where your blood comes from is where your space is
I've seen the bright get duller
I'm not going to spend my life being a color...
If you're thinking of being my brother It don't matter if you're black or white

Michael Jackson, Black or White, HIStory album

The short film to this song has caused worldwide controversies. Due to associative thinking and due to the collective trance it was deemed anti-Semitic by critics and the public, because in the lyrics appears a word which is not found in the dictionary - kike – and it was interpreted as expletive for Jews. Michael Jackson was shocked by this judgment of "small minds," because one who really listens - instead of only hearing - to the song and really observes the film - instead of only looking at it - will not miss the message. Michael Jackson tells us regarding this:

It is not anti-Semitic because I'm not a racist. I could never be a racist. I love all races - from Arabs to Jewish people...to Blacks.
Michael Jackson, Prime Time Live with Diane Sawyer, 1995

I love people of all races from my heart, with true affection.
Michael Jackson, Oprah Winfrey Show, 10th of Feb. 1993

In a conversation with Middle Eastern children from seven to twelve that took place probably in Casablanca, Morocco (or Tunisia), Michael answered a question about his attitude towards racism:

It is a cruelty, it's ugly and I hate it. You are my brothers (points out to the children). They are my brothers. If you are Black, White, Arab...we are all the same. I love all races equally. ... I love Arabs, I love ALL people of the world.
Michael Jackson, www.michaeljackson.ru

Every country is a part of the mansion planet Earth....When we have this wide sight humanity will be one in Spirit....The caste of humanity, the religion of love and the language of the heart - that is it for what I am standing up for.
Sathya Sai Baba, Sanathana Sarathi, 12/1997*

When you don't love humanity, your heart cannot love God. When you condemn your brother man you cannot worship God at the same time. When you do it God will not accept such hypocrisy. God is living in every heart; so when you

serve everyone then this service will reach the God within them. This will bring you the grace of God.
Sathya Sai Baba, Sanathana Sarathi 12/1997*

In the poem "The Magical Child" Michael Jackson describes his vision for the Earth:

The magical child was ready to bow...with silent perfection under God's direction to sing together as one race, stem the tide, transform this place.
Michael Jackson, Magical Child, part 2, Dancing the Dream

This magical child we find in everyone, but it is dominated by a twisted mind and repressed from the head, whose connection to the heart is interrupted and repressed. Thus the access to the wider and more loving parts of our being is blocked.

The goal of Jesus' advent and mission on Earth was the annihilation of the separation between different ethnic groups, races, classes, clans and walks of life. He taught us that the seed of Abraham is only related to bodies. "That is, it is not the children of the flesh who are children of God, but the children of the promise are regarded as descendants." (*Romans 9:8*) He proclaimed: "Very truly I tell you...before Abraham was born I am." (*John 8:58*)

This "I" is the Divine principle inside. This "I" is the essence of man which has to be known and realized. This "I" has nothing in common with the "i."

Jesus came to annihilate the principle of separation, which is characteristic of the antique religions, and replace it by the "religion of love." The law of vengeance that dominates the Old Testament should give way to the law of love. The Sermon on the Mount is an eloquent example for this vision. The early Christians have not yet understood this visionary message, but founded a new religion according to the old patterns of separation. A splitting was never Jesus' purpose, because he was free of prejudices and saw no differences and wanted to realize the brotherhood of man with the fatherhood of God. Even today this high ideal is difficult to understand for most people and yet we can observe that the number of those that are matured for this step to release the old patterns is growing. The law of the race religions says: "An eye for an eye and a tooth for a tooth." The time has come to climb one step higher and replace it by the principle of the "religion of love." "You shall love your neighbor as yourself." Also Sathya Sai Baba has been repeating this message for more than fifty years:

There is only one race, the race of humanity.
Sathya Sai Baba

This race is the brotherhood of man with the fatherhood of God. This ideal was already manifested on Earth during the time of Atlantis and Lemuria. It can manifest now in the same way, when human thinking is elevated above borders and turns divine. "People spoke one language....Atlantis means a universal folk which spoke an universal language, which was spoken on the whole Earth from one race and one folk. They lived like one folk and in a way as a family." (*Spalding, Vol. 6, p. 71**)

15.   The Power of Thoughts

Even as a little boy Michael Jackson was aware of the universal principles
which reign over life, of the power of imagination and thought, and
started early to put into practice the principle, "Man is what he thinks."

Ever since I was a little boy, I had dreamed of creating the biggest-
selling record of all time. I remember going swimming as a child and
making a wish before I jumped into the pool... I wanted to do
something special. I'd stretch my arms out, as if I were sending my
thoughts right up into space. I'd make my wish, then I'd dive into the
water. I'd say to myself: "This is my dream, this is my wish" every time
I'd dive into the water.

I believe in wishes and in a person's ability to make a wish come true. I
really do. Whenever I saw a sunset, I would quietly make my secret
wish right before the sun tucked under the western horizon and
disappeared. I would seem as if the sun had taken my wish with it. I'd
make it right before that last speck of light vanished. And a wish is
more than a wish, it's a goal. It's something your conscious and
subconscious can help make reality.
Michael Jackson, Moonwalk, p. 180f

Michael Jackson formulates here the laws of the process of creation. He
knows the phase of precipitation from energy to matter and applies them.
This law has its roots in the fact that the universe has a very own
intelligence in itself which reacts to our intentions. The results of the
research of biologist Rupert Sheldrake support this knowledge. Starting
with the results of chaos research, physics, ecology and theology he
outlines a unified sight of nature. He found that the universe is traversed
by not local fields, which build an invisible structure and are the reason for
the formation of forms. He calls them morphogenetic fields. He talks

about a "memory of nature," which functions according to the principle of morphogenetic resonance and has no base in material traces. Willing intentions in the form of the power of imagination and thoughts, changes in the morphogenetic fields can be aroused which result in changes in the physical realm.

This insight can be verified by participating observation, but not by distanced observation. Quantum physics has proved the subjectivity of reality on the subatomic level. The physician John Bell formulated the law that confirms these assumptions: Bell's theorem. It says that atomic units that are connected once will stay connected forever. This is not only valid for elementary particles, but also for thoughts, as the basis of both is a vibrating energy field.
"Our thoughts and unconscious persuasions are flying through the world like magnetic prayers, whereupon the environment tries to give us what we seemingly need so urgently." (*Redfield, 1998, p. 142**)

Courageous scientists initiated the turnaround and are bringing back the knowledge of the liveliness and holiness of nature. Aldous Huxley got to the heart of it: **"God is**." We are here to realize this. The ways to this realization are as numerous as the life streams on this planet. The goal is always: "Know thyself," a challenge to remember one's holiness which will lead to healing.

Many hints and support were given to the world by Jesus. The New Testament is not a theologian book with bookish theories and for long overcome traditions, and also not a collection of historical events without relevance and meaning for today's man, but a handbook for physical, emotional and mental healing, a guidebook for our daily life that is, contrary to today's usual handbooks, based on eternal law and timeless principles. It is so modern and timely, of such enormity and foresight, that it is far ahead of our time and is even now not understood by many people. Jesus reveals us the timeless wisdom that there is only one power that can make a real difference and bring about healing - the power of love. It is not easy for a power-obsessed mind to admit that it is totally powerless in front of love. Especially the people of the Western world, who divide the world into two halves, into East and West, and look at their own half as the right one, fail despicably all along the line. He will not fail to come to the insight that only when both halves are fitted to each other, head and heart, outer eye and inner eye, will understanding dawn. Jesus, who was the embodiment of higher knowledge, knew about the delusion of his disciples: "I have much more to say to you, more than you can now bear." (*John 16:12*)

Now after 2000 years man should dare to take the next step of evolution, use his power of discrimination and orient his life and doing in accordance with the law - in Sanskrit Dharma - instead of continuing to follow hypnotic programs, the brainwashing and the congealed patterns of feeling and thinking.

The law of balance which says that we have to reap what we have sown operates mercilessly and impersonally. Whoever seeds tomatoes will harvest tomatoes and whoever seeds matter will find matter, as well as the one who seeds love will harvest love and one who seeds hate will harvest hate. The difficulty in understanding this law, whose action we can observe in the case of the tomato every year again, is the fact that in the case of man it does not work in a yearly cycle, but the time of ripeness is not predictable. Due to lack of knowledge about the inescapability of the harvest, man is keen to lead a simple and comfortable life and uses much time and energy to ensure his material well-being.

Material knowledge enables man to live a comfortable life, to earn his living and to get out of the way of the difficulties of this world. But this knowledge is unworthy of the term "knowledge" - called vidya in Sanskrit. Vidya means that what brings you light opens the eye of wisdom. Because ignorance is darkness....Thus ignorance tries to obtain reputation under the cloak of scientific research.
Sathya Sai Baba, Summer Showers 2*

Instead of striving for wisdom, man is struggling to pile up more and more worldly knowledge. He is engaged in exploring the darkness and is wondering that he does not see. Worldly knowledge is ever changing; wisdom and truth are timeless and unchangeable. Wisdom is realization of the truth. What is true is unchangeable. What changes cannot be true.

Sathya Sai Baba asks the decisive question on which scientists are stuck for an answer even today.

When men can travel to the moon can't they then also start on the journey to the heart?
Sathya Sai Baba, Sanathana Sarathi, 11/1997*

"The truth will set you free" (John 8:32) was the promise which Jesus gave us. The longing for freedom and peace is inherent in every human being from the beginning. Yet he does not recognize that in this search he is searching in the wrong places. He does not know which consequences his actions have. He is rushing for diverting pleasures and yet does not find the longed-for inner peace and thus never reaches his goal. He does not succeed in releasing destructive emotions because his emotional body, in contrast to his physical body, is underdeveloped. The true man is located on higher levels of feeling, of the level of empathy, of unconditional love, of mercy, of faith and forgiving.

16.   Squaring the Circle

The knowledge about material facts is the field of action of academic science. Knowledge in this connection is persuasion and belief, which is deduced by conclusions from observed data. These conclusions are subjective, mirror the consciousness of the observer and say nothing about reality. The history of science shows that to every proved thesis there exists also a proved antithesis. It is a question of general agreement, of a "majority vote" and the dominating collective trance, which theory is accepted as valid and which is rejected.

In science the same principle is in effect as in the shaping of the public opinion in society. What is seen to be the truth is what the majority believes, and this majority is the mediocrity, just as with the population of scientists.

Now this material knowledge is indeed far away from true knowledge. When someone sees with the heart he recognizes the truth intuitively, because he already contains it within himself and a resonance is generated with the encountered truth that had been forgotten for a while. Forgotten stuff can every time, and like a flash of lightning, reach consciousness. This intuitive knowledge is wisdom. It transcends the material realms and cannot be reached by the methods of academic science. Wisdom does not measure, wisdom does not count, wisdom does not weigh something, wisdom does not judge. It unfolds as a result of the exploratory journey inwards, to the spiritual heart, and it cannot be taught.

In mathematics the squaring of the circle is seen as a task without solution, because the transformation of a circle into a square of equal area with geometric means - that is with compass and ruler - is not possible. In analytic geometry the "squaring of the circle" is impossible because it is attempted at the gross level, or as it is called by David Bohm the field of the "first implicit order." This field is superimposed by another layer, a type of "super field" or field of information, which organizes the initial field. This is called the "second super implicit order" and is the principle which organizes the void. The second super implicit order corresponds to the morphogenetic field discovered by Rupert Sheldrake. We can consider everything which exists on three levels:

1. on the level of the explicit,
2. on the level of the implicit and
3. on the level of the super implicit, the void.

The psychologist Stephen Wolinsky deals in his "Quantum Psychology" and in the "Tao of the Chaos" with the third level, where "everything is energy" is valid.

The psychotherapist Bert Hellinger also reaches, in his method of family constellations, the level of the super implicit. On this level information reveals itself directly when the person is centered, con-centrated and aware. This attitude is very difficult for Western people, because due to socialization they are nearly unable to release judgment, analysis and interpretation and to take everything the way it is, to agree to everything as it reveals itself.

The physicist Stephen Hawking is searching for the world formula or a coherent theory of experiencing and behaving. This can never be found on the level of the explicit, because that is the level of multiplicity and separation. A coherent theory has to focus on unity which leads beyond the implicit level to the void.

We can illustrate the characteristics of the three levels by referring to modern computer technology. With the help of tiny light points, every form can be produced without any difficulty; everything can be morphed to everything in no time. From space are morphed forms and forms are transformed in space. Space is energy. With a computer the squaring of a circle is a piece of cake, and also for our spirit, if we focus it on the level of energy, of void, of space. Energy is the base and fundament of everything that exists. While energy is formless and all-encompassing, by ordering this amorphous energy forms are created, while the energy is blocked in the form as long as the form exists. It cannot be used to create new forms before the form is dissolved. The void, free-floating energy, which is present before every forming is what the wise, holy and enlightened people call consciousness, as absolute pure consciousness, as spirit. This spirit is identical to the Holy Ghost of Christianity. Michael

Jackson reveals in his lyrics that he has access to these realms of being and knows the source.

Once you were lost
but now you are home
in a nonlocal Universe
There is nowhere to go
From Here to Here
Is the Unbounded
Ocean of Consciousness
We are like ripples
In the Sea of Bliss
Michael Jackson, Heaven is Here, Dancing the Dream

In "Mother" he talks about his existence before any form:
Eons of time I've been gestating
To take a form been hesitating
From the unmanifest this cosmic conception
On this earth a fantastic reception
And then on a fateful August morn
From your being I was born
With tender love you nurtured a seed
To your own distress you paid no heed
Unmindful of any risk and danger
You decided upon this lonely stranger
Michael Jackson, Mother, Dancing the Dream

Michael Jackson recognizes the unlimited ocean of consciousness as our identity, and the impossibility of travel from one place to another, because we are not limited forms which can move forward, but because we embrace the whole space, we are the primal ground of all forms and permeate all forms and all no-forms.

On the level of the super implicit order, space and particles consist of the same substance, whereby space and particles differ only in relation to density. When space, alias energy, reaches a certain density, is composed sufficiently, a particle appears. There is no qualitative difference between energy and particle.

This knowledge enters consciousness during a journey inwards. All concepts, structures and imaginations are dissolved, so that there no longer exists a separation between space and particle; the "substance" of space and particle is mingled. The borders between inside and outside, between thing and not-thing, nothing, between object and no-object are dissolved. This primal substance, or better, the emerging energy field, is without order, chaotic, unstructured, free of concepts. Michael Jackson describes this process of creation:

All this hysteria, all this commotion

Time, space, energy are just a notion

What we have conceptualized we have created

All those loved, all those hated

Michael Jackson, Breaking Free, Dancing the Dream

Michael's words remind us of a jailbreak, which he titled "Breaking free." Did he talk about a jailbreak or a freebreak? In the song "You are not alone" he also expresses that distance is only a concept of mind, but not a reality:

You are not alone

I am here with you

though you're far away...

You're always in my heart,

for you are not alone

Michael Jackson, You are not alone, HIStory album

Who knows if Michael Jackson is talking about the "I" or about the "i," the ego, if he means his physical heart or his spiritual heart? Richard Bach expresses it in his most enchanting story, "There's No Such Place as Far Away," the following way: "Fly free and happy beyond birthdays and across forever, and we'll meet now and then when we wish, in the midst of the one celebration that can never end." (Bach, 1992*)

The dissolution of particles in space can be compared to the dissolution of waves in the ocean. The wave emerges for a moment from the surface of the ocean, rises and takes a form, moves on and is separated for some time from the neighbor wave and the ocean until it ebbs away and disappears in the ocean again. Before and after the appearance there is no separation; the wave and the ocean are one. The name wave has no meaning and what was the form of a wave for a short time has merged into the formless.

The "Course in Miracles" offers a one-year-practice to reach wisdom, to reach the inner certainty of oneness. The first four lessons are:
1. Nothing I See In This Room (on this street, from this window, in this place) Means Anything;
2. I Have Given Everything I See In This Room (on this street, from this window, in this place) All The Meaning That It Has For Me;
3. I Do Not Understand Anything I See In This Room (on this street, from this window, in this place); and
4. These Thoughts Do Not Mean Anything. They Are Like The Things I See In This Room (on this street, from this window, in this place). (Course in Miracles, The Workbook, pages 3-7).

The water being a wave believes itself to be a separate entity from the ocean; as soon as the wave merges into the ocean the wave no longer exists. The water with the identity of "wave" and without identity is the same. With the loss of identity nothing changed; only the form dissolved and the name became meaningless.

Man has been driven since prehistoric times by the longing for freedom, yet paradoxically he is continuously building his own prison and chains himself. The chains are like concepts, imaginations and identities, which he creates. Every created identity produces a border and separation. These identities we call personality. The personality is all that which defines our specialty, divides and separates us from others, makes us solitary and causes joy and sorrow, in short: the ego. This ego is a product of the illusion of the mind and not real.

The personality, the limited ego, has to die when man wants to be free instead of believing that his prison is freedom. Every imagining of ourselves ties us. One who imagines himself to be a sinner is tied to the concept of a sinner. One who imagines himself to be superior is tied to the concept of superiority-inferiority. One who imagines that life is hard will feel the hardness.

When the ego, the identification with the human "I" has disappeared, one does not feel superior and not inferior.
Sathya Sai Baba Speaks, p. 260*

The ideal of many nations, which is formulated in the constitution, "Liberty, Equality, Fraternity" can only be realized when man lets go of his identification with parts of the whole and with roles. Michael Jackson dances in his short film "Black or White" on the Statue of Liberty, which faces every incomer in the haven of New York with the silent message of the longed-for freedom. At the feet of the statue of the lady who holds the burning torch, we find the inscription:

The new Colossus
Not like the brazen giant of Greek fame
with conquering limbs astride from land to land
Here at our sea-washed, sunset gates shall stand
A mighty woman with a torch, whose flame
is the imprisoned lightning, and her name
Mother of Exiles. From her beacon-hand
Glows world-wide welcome; her mild eyes command
The air-bridged harbor that twin cities frame.
"Keep ancient lands, your storied pomp!" cries she
with silent lips. "Give me your tired, your poor,
your huddled masses yearning to breathe free,
the wretched refuse of your teeming shore.

92

Send these, the homeless, tempest-tost to me,
I lift my lamp beside the Golden door!
(Emma Lazarus, cit. in Book of Life, p. 240)

Michael Jackson shares this vision of unity and liberty:

We have come to celebrate here
The getting rid of every fear
Of every notion, every seed
Of any separation, caste or creed.
Michael Jackson, Ecstasy, Dancing the Dream

Only when we have let go all these races, classes, religions and groupings as well as patterns of believing and persuasions are we freed from the ties of space and time.

When you are locked in a pattern of thinking and responding, your creativity gets blocked. You miss the freshness and magic of the moment. Learn to be innocent again, and that freshness never fades.
Michael Jackson, Innocence, Dancing the Dream

Life exists only in the here and now, in the presence. The presence is free from patterns, structures, concepts and blockades. The presence is.

Jesus' last words on the cross were not: "My God, my God, why have you forsaken me?," but "My God, my God, you never let me or one of your children down, because your children can come to you as I came to you. They can see my life as I lived my life. By living this life like this, they can embody the Christ and become One with You, God my Father." (Spalding, Vol. 6, p. 76*)

17. Wisdom

We have called attention to the difference between material knowledge and wisdom. Material knowledge comes from the mind and takes up an impersonal attitude towards the object of the knowledge. Wisdom comes from the spiritual heart and takes up a sympathetic attitude.
What is imparted by wisdom seems to be paradoxical to the measuring and judging mind. Wisdom belongs to the realms of quality, not quantity. It originates with the perception and awareness of the holiness and liveliness of creation and adopts an attitude of dignity and reverence. Such vocabulary is strange to academic science, because it does not explore the deep but only measures the lowlands.

Michael Jackson's story, "So the Elephants March," is a lesson from the bottom. The elephant is a symbol for those who sweeps barriers out of the way and slashes the way through the jungle.

"What fear and anger this creature (man) has," the elephants thought. "But he is going to inherit the earth. We are wise enough to see that. Let us set an example for him."..."Let us show them our reverence for life," they said. ... So the elephants march on, and every tread beats out words in the dust. "Watch, learn, love. Watch, learn, love." Can you hear them?
Michael Jackson, So the Elephants March, Dancing the Dream

The story of "The Boy and the Pillow" also illustrates that wisdom comes to different results than the limited greedy monkey mind, as it is called by the Americans. Mind of the monkey because the mind jumps restless like a monkey from branch to branch, that means from on thought to the next. It doesn't come to rest, is unable to center itself and is distracted by everything that comes its way.

A wise father wanted to teach his young son a lesson...."Are you mad?" his father said. "When is one piece of silver worth more than fifty gold ducats?" "When it's offered out of love," the boy replied...."You have lost your wits completely," his father said, shaking his head. "When is a penny worth more than a piece of silver?" "When it's offered out of devotion," the boy replied....At this the wise father smiled and embraced his son, and with a tear in his eye he murmured, "You have learned well."
Michael Jackson, The Boy and the Pillow, Dancing the Dream

"More than 25 centuries have passed since what is called the Eternal Wisdom was for the first time entrusted in the writings....In Vedanta, in the prophecies of the Old Testament, in the Tao Te Ching, in the dialogues of Plato, in the Gospels of John, in the Mahayana theology, with Plotinus and the Aeropagus, with the Persian Sufis and the Christian Mystics of the Middle Age ... the Eternal Wisdom has spoken." (Bhagavad Gita, p. 13)

The truth has been spoken out and promulgated ever since and yet people are closing their mind for it, as was said by Galilei: "Verily, just as serpents close their ears, so do these men close their eyes to the light of truth." (Letter to Kepler)

This truth can be found inside of everyone and the path thereto is linked with some efforts.   Thus most people prefer the easy way without guessing that the worldly way is easy in the beginning and then turns ever more difficult, while the way to wisdom and truth is difficult at the beginning and then turns ever easier. Rememberers are trying to describe a truth that is indescribable due to its very essence. It will never be figured out by deduction, but only by immediate recognition, which transcends the mind.

Herrmann Hesse describes in his Indian poetry "Siddhartha" from 1920 this way of initiation: "With the exception of one small thing, one tiny little thing, they lacked nothing that the sage and thinker had, and that was the consciousness of the unity of all life. Within Siddhartha there slowly grew and ripened the knowledge of what wisdom really was and the goal of his long seeking." (Hesse, p. 90, wikiquote.org)

When man learns by wisdom instead of by fear and doubt he can safe himself from much suffering. Then he does not learn because there is no other way, but because he wants always to climb new heights and follows the urge to reach the peak. This longing for the peak is an authentic desire of the soul, contrary to the artificially adopted desires of the personality. Artificial desires are defense mechanisms against growth and the fulfillment of the goal and purpose of being human.

Sathya Sai Baba tells us the story of an exemplary mother:
In the city of Calcutta lived a mother with her son. The mother made many sacrifices to afford the education for her son. Thereby she imprinted on him the following statement: "Don't care about worldly education. Foolish people are graduating in all sort of academic fields, but don't know who they are. Only by studying can man get rid of his lower characteristics. By scholarship man learns how to deal with controversies, but does not reach complete wisdom. For what reason should man finish studies which will only end with death? One should study that which will free man from death. Only spiritual knowledge will lead to immortality. Only that will last....For that reason, dear son, start the spiritual search during your studies."
Sathya Sai Baba erzählt, chap. 12*

18.   The Purpose of Existence

Michael Jackson sees himself as an instrument. An instrument does not act out of its own will, but it serves the one who uses and leads it. It serves to express something or to convey a message. A messenger is sent with a message. He is not the originator of the same and does not act out of his own interest. He is the medium of the one who employs his services. From childhood Michael Jackson felt that he was an instrument which was used by something higher, which was connecting with the world through his music and dance. Oprah Winfrey comments in relation to Michael Jackson: "An instrument of nature, that's an interesting way to describe yourself....Are you very spiritual?...I mean, do you, do you meditate? Do you understand that there is something bigger than yourself at work here?" Michael answers:

I believe in God, absolutely, absolutely, very much.
Michael Jackson, Oprah Winfrey Interview, 10th Feb. 1993

Two years later Michael again confirms in the Diana Sawyer show and in a Simulchat his view:

I believe in spirituality and I believe in a higher source, such as God.
Michael Jackson, Diana Sawyer Show, 14th June 1995

I pray that we continue to serve the world in a positive way, not a negative way, and not hurt anyone, because it's wonderful.
Michael Jackson, Simulchat, 17th Aug. 1995

He does not use the superlatives which the world has conferred to him to inflate his ego, but stays true to himself, even when the world does not understand him. To the question of how it feels to him to be a real king, he answers:

I never try to think hard about it because I don't want it to go to my head.

Michael Jackson, Ebony, 1992

If we consider the many stars whose fame went to their head it is amazing that **the** megastar of the late second millenium - the "King of Pop," the "American Master," as C. Mecca called him, the "Musik-Meister" as he was titled in German on 25nd of Feb. 1998 on the news channel CNN, when he was part of 4000 invited guests of honor participating at the festivities in Seoul at the swearing-in ceremony of the elected south Korean president Kim Dae-jung, does not raise any claim to be the maker. He declares instead:

Talent is something that God gives to a person....Ed Sullivan...told me, "Never forget where your talent came from, that your talent is a gift from God."...but I could have told him that my mother had never let me forget....she instilled in me a love of Him that I will always have.

Michael Jackson, Moonwalk, p. 29, 13, 14, 12

I am honored that I have this ability. I thank God for it every day. I try to cultivate what He gave me. I feel I am compelled to do what I do.

Michael Jackson, Moonwalk, p. 272

He refuses the laurels with which they want to crown him and leaves the honor to God and to nature. Ancient principles of wisdom say: "The greatest among you will be your servant. For those who exalt themselves will be humbled, and those who humble themselves will be exalted." *(Matthew 23:11-12)*
"But many who are first will be last, and many who are last will be first." *(Matthew 19:30)*

The principles of the Gospels are valid and independent from zeitgeist. Do we really understand the deeper meaning? They don't relate to outer fame, but characterize the inner greatness of someone. A real great soul - mahatma in Sanskrit – is not concerned about pomp and splendor, but acts in stillness knowing himself to be the instrument of God.

When I think of my mother and our early years, I can tell you there are rewards that go far beyond money and public acclaim and awards.
Michael Jackson, Moonwalk, p. 14

Michael Jackson believes that everyone on this planet is here for a special task and with a certain purpose.

I believe that everybody comes to the world for a reason.
Michael Jackson, Oprah Winfrey interview, 10th Feb. 1992

I really believe that God chooses people to do certain things, the way Michelangelo or Leonardo da Vinci or Mozart or Muhammad Ali or Martin Luther King is chosen. And that is their mission to do that thing. And I think that I haven't scratched the surface yet of what my real purpose is for being here. I'm committed to my art. I

believe that all art has as its ultimate goal the union between the material and the spiritual, the human and the Divine. And I believe that that is the very reason for the existence of art and what I do.
Michael Jackson, Ebony, May 1992

Union between the human and the Divine means that these are like the two sides of a medal; one side cannot exist without the other side. Sathya Sai Baba came to earth to awaken humanity to this knowledge. The union between the material and the spiritual is not only the purpose of art, but the goal of any human Dasein (being) on this earth. Everybody can reach this goal. Sathya Sai Baba shows us the way:

Man nowadays does not recognize his human nature. How shall they then recognize their innate divinity? Only when man is aware of his humanity will he be able to recognize his divinity.
Sathya Sai Baba, Sanathana Sarathi, 02/1998*

Only when our life is governed by dharma, the eternal law, can the ideals of equality, brotherhood and liberty be realized.
Sathya Sai Baba, Sanathana Sarathi, 11/1997*

As Michael Jackson had limitless compassion from an early age. He recognized early that his task was to care about needy people in this world. He considered caring for children and active collaboration in healing this wounded planet as his duty. He heard the cries for help and dedicated himself relentlessly. Not under public view, but silently and unrecognized he followed the call of his heart. "They don't know him as a pop star. For them he is only a nice guy, who came here to bring hope," was the comment to Michael's visit of an orphanage in Thailand in November 1996. Michael Jackson knew how urgently help is needed:

We have to heal our wounded world....I want my work to help people rediscover the child that's hiding in them.

Michael Jackson, On Children of the World, Dancing the Dream

Each child is perfect at birth. Under the influence of the elders with their twisted and limited minds he removes himself from this perfection.

You have come to this world to reach God. Through ignorance of this fact you have loaded the weight of illusion on your head.
Sathya Sai Baba Speaks, Vol. 2*)

19. Music of the Spheres

Also other artists have used the image of the instrument or the channel to explain how their music comes up. From John Lennon the following is recorded:

When the real music comes to me - the music of the spheres, the music that surpasseth understanding - that has nothing to do with me 'cause I'm just the channel. The only joy for me is for it to be given to me and transcribe it. Like a medium. Those moments are what I live for.
John Lennon, cit. in Michael Jackson, Moonwalk, introduction

Michael Jackson describes his own experience:
People ask me how I make music. I tell them I just step into it. It's like stepping into a river and joining the flow. Every moment in the river has its song. So I stay in the moment and listen....When you join the flow, the music is inside and outside, and both are the same. As long as I can listen to the moment, I'll always have music.
Michael Jackson, How I Make Music, Dancing the Dream

One who opens up for inspiration and intuition connects to a higher source of wisdom and thus creates his message from this source. He becomes a channel for the deeper layers of being, which are not available to the mind and the thinking in concepts. Michael says about the preparations of his performance of "Billie Jean" during the festivities of the 25th anniversary of Motown on 16th May 1983:

I was there by myself, the night before the show, and I pretty much stood there and let the song tell me what to do. I kind of let the dance

create itself. I really let it *talk* to me; I heard the beat come in...letting the "Billie Jean" rhythm create the movements. I felt almost compelled to let it create itself. I couldn't help it. And that - being able to "step back" and let the dance come through - was a lot of fun.
Michael Jackson, Moonwalk, p. 209f

Similar was the experience of composing "Earth Song":
I remember writing "Earth Song" when I was in Austria, in a hotel. And I was feeling so much pain and so much suffering of the plight of the Planet Earth. And for me, this is Earth's Song, because I think nature is trying so hard to compensate for man's mismanagement of the Earth. And with the ecological unbalance going on, and a lot of the problems in the environment, I think Earth feels the pain, and she has wounds, and it's about some of the joys of the planet as well. But this is my chance to pretty much let people hear the voice of the planet. And this is "Earth Song." And that's what inspired it. And it just suddenly dropped into my lap when I was on tour in Austria.
Michael Jackson, HIStory Museum, www.mjjfc.com in 1999, now: www.songfacts.com

"Stranger in Moscow" got to him, because that day he felt in that way:
In 1994 I wrote "Stranger in Moscow" - a song about a very difficult period in my life. It was difficult not only because of what was going on actually, but I was very lonely for a very long time. I was freezing.
Michael Jackson, Official Photobook My World, cit. on www.all4michael.com

103

John Lennon considers such moments of inspiration as highlights in his life. What is that, the real music, the music of the spheres, the music beyond mind?

In all creation accounts of all cultures and in the holy scriptures of all countries we find the view that the world was made of sound. The Gospels begin with: "In the beginning was the word, and the word was with God, and the word was God." *(John 1:1)*

In the Veda, the holy scriptures of India, which are dated between the year 1500 B.C. and 1500 A.C. it is said in the Aitareya-Aranyaka, 4:8: In the beginning all this verily was Atman only, one and without a second. There was nothing else that winked. He bethought Himself, "Let Me now create the worlds." He created these worlds, the world of water-bearing clouds, the world of the solar ray, the world of mortals and the world of waters. *(Churchward, p. 29 and www.consciouslivingfoundation.org)* "And furthermore it is said, "nâdabrahman," which means, "Everything is sound." In Sanskrit the meaning vibrates in the sound of the words and syllables, whose impact unfolds when our mind is unaware. By the vibration of the sound, a resonance originates in the deeper aspects of being. "Nâdabrahman" is the representation of the nameless Absolute - brahman - in his first manifestation as sound. The symbol for this representation is the sign for the primal vibe OM, which became AMEN in Christianity, in Islam became ALLA HU AKBAR, and in Sikhism, EK OM KAR." *(Gooi, p. 341*)*

OM is the sound of the movement of the stars in the sky; it is the sound which manifested when the dawn of the creative will prompted the featureless to activity. There are endless subtle fine sounds, which no ear can hear. Therefore you can understand that the sound OM was produced as the elements came to existence and creation began. This sound is the primordial, the primeval One. Sathya Sai Baba Speaks, Vol. 5*

The musicologist and master of "inner hearing," Joachim-Ernst Berendt, published various fascinating books and music albums relating to this issue. He shows us the way to the music of life, which is made of sounds and becomes hearable when one listens inwardly instead of directing the senses outwards. The dimension "sound" is a continuum which reaches from "audible sound" to "stillness." As illustrated by the yin-yang symbol, all existence consists of poles which are not opposites but complementary, which means that they complement each other and manifest in a cyclic permanent alternation, wavelike, incessantly vibrating. The poles of the dimension of sound are audible sound and inaudible stillness, whereby the stillness also has the quality of sound and the sound contains the quality of stillness in itself. From this stillness, true music rises to the wave peak and becomes audible until it merges again in the wave trough and fades away.

The world has replaced the poles, "audible sound" and "stillness," with the opposites, "noise" and "outer silence." Silence is not automatically stillness, because it only means that noise is absent, that there is nothing to hear with the outer ears. But that does not mean stillness, because the inner ear is still hearing the stream of thoughts which is incessantly in uproar. This silence is illusory because the noise of mind continues and is still perceptible.

Some people are able to retreat so far from the noise of the world that they can enjoy the music of the spheres. The few who are able to hear with the Inner Ear describe their experience as follows: "Every ascended being of light sends out an individual key note, which is embedded in a beautiful symphony of sounds. And while it is moving through interstellar space, the mixture of its cosmic sounds represents an inspiration for all who have the privilege of access to the skills of the Inner Ear." *(Book of Life, p. 204*)*

"We were informed that we were able to hear the music every time we were getting still. ... We were informed that this music is that which is called choir of angels. They call it the "Symphony of Souls Unison." *(Spalding, Vol. I, p. 130*)*

Sathya Sai Baba confirms: *Only in the depth of silence can the word of God be heard.*
Sathya Sai Baba, Upanishad Vahini, Cover*

And Friedrich Nietzsche wrote: "The way to all the great goes through the stillness."

Michael Jackson shares his experience:
My dance is all motion without, all silence within. As much as I love to make music, it's the unheard music that never dies. And silence is my real dance, though it never moves.
Michael Jackson, Dance of Life, Dancing the Dream

"The natural songs of the sun, the planets, the host of angels and the ascended masters are - like the scent of flowers - the radiance of those beings...which contribute to the music of spheres, because each one of them could concentrate on the gift of singing...or the gift of music, which was developed by the special talents of their self-conscious intelligence, and focus their attention on it." *(Book of Life, p. 204*)*

Michael Jackson concentrated on his talents by dedicating his whole life to music, the most efficient method for awakening the sleeping consciousness of mankind. Music is compared to the spoken word as a method of transformation, its invaluable advantage that it circumvents the resistance of the mind and reaches realms of our being, which are more open for unusual and new things than our thinking.

Through the rhythm and harmony of sound, a resonance with the source of life is created, so that the message which is transported by the vehicle of music can reach the depth of our soul directly, without the diversion of the separating logic of the mind and reason, which are ruled by the ego. Every time the common thinking system is doubted, the mind panics, because it fears the loss of its illusive security and order. Everything has to be fought against which does not fit in its scheme. It develops fierce resistance and tries to avert the supposed danger by aggression. The mind does not understand that aggression will return to him like a boomerang sooner or later. "In the moment you combat a thing you combat yourself! Be always on guard when the destructive element is discussed." *(Yo soy*)*

Even when hearing the very truth the mind behaves in this crazy way. The most simple way to cheat it is to address the feeling, not the sentimental feeling, which puts us in trance, but the fellow feeling, the compassion of the souls, which don't identify with the ego and are not led by it but by the inner divine source. We reach the source when we direct the senses inward and enter stillness. From stillness then emerges the music of the spheres. Michael Jackson describes his personal experiences in an interview with the magazine "Ebony" in 1992:

I feel fortunate for being that instrument through which music flows. I'm just the source through which it comes. I can't take credit for it because it's God's work....Deep inside I feel that this world we live in is really a big, huge, monumental symphonic orchestra. I believe that in its primordial form all of creation is sound and that it's not just random sound, that it's music. You've heard the expression, music of the spheres? Well, that's a very literal phrase. In the Gospels we

107

read: "And the Lord God made man from the dust of the earth and breathed into his nostrils the breath of life and man became a living soul." That breath of life to me is the music of life and it permeates every fiber of creation. In one of the pieces of the Dangerous album I say: "Life songs of ages throbbing in my blood, have danced the rhythm of the tide and flood." This is a very literal statement, because the same new miracle intervals and biological rhythms that sound out the architecture of my DNA also governs the movement of the stars. The same music governs the rhythm of the seasons, the pulse of our heartbeats, the migration of birds, the ebb and flow of ocean tides, the cycles of growth, evolution and dissolution. It's music, it's rhythm. And my goal in life is to give to the world what I was lucky to receive: the ecstasy of divine union through my music and my dance. It's like, my purpose, it's what I'm here for.

Michael Jackson, Ebony, May 1992

Michael Jackson's experience confirms the hermetic principle: "As below so above." He understands that man has that which is flowing from the invisible realms to bring to manifestation, in the threefold cycle of everything which will manifest:

1. Creation
2. Preservation and development
3. Dissolution.

After every cycle the next will follow like a spiral and lead to a higher level of consciousness.

A star can never die. It just turns into a smile and melts back into the cosmic music, the dance of life. I like that thought, the last one I have before my eyes close. With a smile, I melt back into the music myself.

Michael Jackson, Dance of Life, Dancing the Dream

The ability to hear this music is latently available in every human being. Michael Jackson says:

Inside your heart sits a Seer

Between his thoughts, he can hear

A melody simple but wondrously clear

The music of life, so precious, so dear

Michael Jackson, Magical Child, Dancing the Dream

This cycle follows a rhythm. We know the rhythm of time, the rhythm of the day, the week, the month and the year, the rhythm of tide and flood. We know how much power is produced when soldiers march in lockstep over a bridge. When they get in resonance with the proper frequency of the bridge they are able to destroy the static of the bridge. Unbroken rhythm means harmony, peace, prosperity, flowing, health. Broken rhythm leads to broken hearts, insanity, dis-ease, dis-peace, misery.

"Music...is a conductor, which never produces...resistance or the feeling of fight. It is a harmonic stream of energy which can regulate outer phenomena and thus change the quality of energy as easily as fire transforms all low vibratory rates and all substance to the fourth dimension, without argument and without fight." (*Book of Life, p. 212**)

The music which is talked about here is the true music, which John Lennon referred to and which Michael Jackson received, because he opened up himself for the harmonies instead of abusing sound for creating dissonant and destructive rhythms. The condition to be able to receive these melodies is that the instrument has to be pure, clear and empty. "When the glorious melody from the holy Christ-Self...flows out from the LOWER VEHICLES THE RESULTING MELODY...DEPENDS ON THE HARMONY INSIDE OF EACH OF THESE VEHICLES." *(Book of Life, p. 210*)*

"I would like to describe to you the **heart of God**. That is a task which I am not able to put veritably into words, but I want at least to incite your interest so far that you will start to travel deeper and deeper with the media of your consciousness into the **stillness,** which forms the holy heart from which this universe and we all come to being....It is as still as the sun in the heavens fulfilling its cosmic duties and yet it is filled with sound in perfect harmony." *(Book of Life, p. 172*)*

In the holy Indian scriptures the avatar Krishna is often presented with a flute playing enchanting melodies. Sathya Sai Baba tells us a story which reveals the secret of this flute:

One day Gauranga prayed to Krishna: "Oh Lord, won't you tell me the secret to how I can become dear to you and can come near to you? How lucky is this flute!" In this night Lord Krishna appeared in his dream and said: "Gauranga, when you have become an instrument like this flute, through which my breath is flowing and divine music is resounding, then explore the flute a little bit more closely. It is hollow; inside is nothing. When I blow my breath in it, it flows freely through it and produces enchanting melodies. Therefore make yourself hollow and make sure to free your heart from all passions and emotions and your mind from all desires. Then I will make you into my instrument for sure. But be alert! There may not be the least vein of ego or attachment in you, because this would hinder the free and easy flow of my breath and there would not come out any beautiful music.
Sathya Sai Baba erzählt, Vol II*

Angels spend their entire lives, which are forever, spinning around the creator's throne, singing His praise.... The harmonies of angelic choirs are incredibly complex, they say, but the rhythm is simple. "It's mostly march time," one eavesdropper affirmed. For some reason, that fact is almost the best I have learned so far.

Michael Jackson, Angel of Light, Dancing the Dream

Working on his new album to be released in 2000, Michael Jackson reaches a new level. Rodney Jerkins, one of his collaborators, cites Michael Jackson in an interview in 1999 with MTV News, USA. It becomes clear that Michael Jackson urges his people to approximate the inside level, which is stillness and which is the source of wisdom and truth. "He (Michael Jackson) sat down and said, 'I want you to give everything you got. Reach for something deeper. Go for it. Anything that you've never done before. Do it again. Do it now. Just go. Just go.'"

(Michael Jackson Taps Rodney Jerkins, David Foster To Produce Next Record by MTV News Staff 3/11/1999; http://www.mtv.com/news/1430441/michael-jackson-taps-rodney-jerkins-david-foster-to-produce-next-record/)

The deeper is something that transcends that which "i" consider to be possible. It is something that "i" believe to be unreachable, what "i" cannot imagine. This "i" is the limited, little, petty "i" or ego, which experiences itself as separated from "I" and denies his true identity. When "i" steps back and leaves the leadership to "I," the music of the spheres is brought to earth and we all can tune in into the choir of angels.

20. i

Each time someone says, "I am such and such," he reduces himself to "suchandsuch," and he limits himself and denies himself. He limits himself without knowing that in reality He is limitless and boundless. He is unable to recognize that he is reducing himself day by day through thoughts and words. Each time man uses the words "I" or "I am" and equates them with less than perfection and Divinity, he is offending his true nature and identifies himself with a label which he has stuck on himself. That is blasphemy.

Man makes himself in his ignorance into something meaningless, ridiculous, marionette-like, and has created a pseudo-i, the ego, to conceal this meaninglessness, ridiculousness and marionette-likeness. Thus he is, throughout his life, cheating himself and feels really great, when accordingly his ego has blown up. Yes he is great, really well behaved. (In German we have a wordplay: großartig = great; groß artig = greatly well behaved). Like a well-behaved child he is following the null ego, which suggests that he is all that is. Aldous Huxley called this pseudo-i "ghoulish distorted gestalt," which Shakespeare has described: "...like an angry ape plays such fantastic tricks before high heaven, as make the angels weep." *(cit. in Huxley, mp. 96, and www.enotes.com)*

Sathya Sai Baba cites in "Clearing of Doubts" an Indian folk song, in which the ego is unmasked as marionette and puppet. He advises his pupil, who is searching for his identity, his Self:
Try to conceive the meaning of this folk dance song....Don't merely read this song, but ponder deeply on the meaning of each word. The song will surely change your thinking....Listen carefully!

1. Thai! Thai! Thai! Marionette
See the ignorant play of this puppet

112

Oh soul, listen to the long, long story
of her past, her future, behind and in front!

2. First it rolled in soft slurry
in mother's womb, its dark prison
It came with a mewl, but all around it
smiled in joy and on feasts in quantities

3. "Oh tragedy! I am born again,"
it knew and cried, loudly and lengthy
But all the time they were caressing it
And laughed to coax a laugh from it

4. During the day it is wallowing in its own filth
without a sense for shame
it stood up and fell at every step
performing daily a childish play

5. It runs and jumps with fellow dudes
Learning hundreds tricks and deals
It turns so big and heavy and wide
From year to year, directly and quickly

6. It merges to couples and whispers
sweet nothings in rosy rainbow style
it sings in melodies never heard before
and fills the cup, unique and strange

7. This brahman who makes these puppets as couples
and puppets and puppets millionfold
but this our puppet does not know
when it is playing with dummies
Thim! Thim! Thim!

8. This delusive puppet has like the bull
the rope of ignorance in its nostrils
Lust and anger are like scorpion wipes
which dash on the back of slaves

9. It is entranced by malicious joy when others
in front of it hick shuddering the bottom
It delivers pain sparingly, but itself
cannot bear the tiniest part of it

10. It swears and yells and swings its arms
and is foaming with rage and blood-red eyes
it is indeed a wondrous sight
obsessed by the devil's rage

11. It scans and writes, it scribbles and crams
The reason why, it does not know
It runs in panic while trying
willy-nilly to collect food for the belly

12. Ah, did you see this funny little marionette
the belly filled with so many books
twisting and wriggling itself, green with envy
when it meets an educated puppet?

13. And you should hear its secret cackle
when an ashamed sensual urge
a wicked lurking voracity
is satisfied in sin

14. it claps itself - where indeed - on its shoulder in pride!
For beauty, muscles, vitality.
Whereby it all the time and step by step
is heading senility

15. *It wavers and squints through wrinkles and frowns*
and when the children shout: "Old ape! Old ape!"
it gapes and grins toothlessly.
Its bones are rattling.

16. *Until the end it is lost in fear, wear and tear*
and many tearful scuffles
What for is, oh marionette, your gasping and groaning
Your needs must be met by fate

17. *Aha, the bird! It beats its wings!*
It frees itself, brrr, from the cage of skin
empty, it stiffens; uninhabited it rectifies
Oh, eliminate it from sight

18. *The elements follow their five parents*
The wishes of the puppet turned to dust and ash
Why cry, you fools, when one of you
falls on the overpopulated stage

19. *Uncles, cousins, aunts and friends*
march in black mood to the room door
the illusionary puppet, ach, forgot its relatives
the Divine Name, the True Savior!

20. *Oh man, don't lean against this slim reed*
Only a sneeze, this weak boat made of skin
equipped with three times three leaks
will let you fall in the midst of the stream

21. *This puppet cries, it sleeps and wakes*
when the strings are pulled by a invisible hand
He is the Lord who stands behind it

But the marionette swears, that am I, I, I

22. Dharma, karma are the tough strings
He tightens them, He loses them
Not aware of this the puppet is strutting
criss-cross on the boards

23. It sees the world as permanent
the folly strutting marionette
in a flash He concludes the show!
Gone are pomp and pride!

24. Oh man, you struggled through
ant, snake and bird
Search for and find without delay
the road to lasting bliss

25. Appreciate your luck! You can now see
Lord Krishna, He has come!
Be related to Him and you will recognize
Your what and why and how

26. One million words, so smart and nice
Are they able to still your gnawing hunger?
Lit instead the light of your soul
and run off, freed from ties and play

27. This song which talks about the marionette
makes man sad and wise! I know
But man! See the great wonder
of Sathya Sai Nâtha
and ....know thyself!
Sathya Sai Baba, Answers, p. 113f*

Who knows himself has dissolved his "i." He knows that this "i" is an illusion, with which he has identified in his ignorance. But as soon there is sufficient light, the illusion will be unmasked and the identity of man will reveal itself.

To reach the state of "the light of the Soul," human consciousness has to reach the higher bodies. It will not arise from outer circumstances, but by abiding at the inner place of peace, which is free from the phenomena of the outer world. But this detachedness from worldly things develops equanimity and serenity. Serenity is a state which does not change, either by luck or misfortune, either by joy or pain, either by gain or loss, either by highs or lows. Whatever may happen in the life of a serene person, he will be uninfluenced in his state of mind or emotional state.

At the same time in the state of serenity there will be revealed regularities of life, creations beyond nature will be possible and the door to wisdom will open. The distinguishing characteristic of such inspirations is that the knowledge just comes to us, jumps into consciousness, preferentially in those moments when we don't think about it, as for instance during sleep, during recreation or during activities which don't require mental effort and when the "i" is not active. In such moments it can happen that knowledge drops quasi in one's lap. Many important inventors have experienced this phenomenon that the crucial ideas came to them in those moments, when they expected it least - travelling, during recreation, while dreaming. An example of this is the chemist Kekulé, who discovered the ring structure of benzene in a dream, when a snake bit itself in its tail.

Michael Jackson confirmed at various times that the composition of his music and films happened in exactly this way. Whoever wants to understand Michael Jackson and his message has to master the lower emotions of the "i" and develop higher emotions, which don't circle around the ego, are not egocentric, but are worldcentric. Otherwise the

117

necessary resonances do not come into existence to tune in to the same field of meaning. When I hear a language which is unknown to me, it cannot produce a resonance in my cells. Even if I listen endlessly to this language, I will understand nothing. One who wants to understand Michael Jackson has to know the language of higher knowledge. This cannot be learned at universities, but by connection with the Self and that what IS. It can rise to consciousness in dreams, in stillness and during meditation, always when the ever-restless mind comes to rest.

Ignorant people deny themselves the possibility of reaching this level of evolution and interpret the experiential reports of the knowing and realized ones as hallucinations or delusions of the mind. They thereby fail to notice that they themselves are deluded by phantasms and mistake the rope on its way in the darkness of the mind for a snake. This false view produces fear and anxiety. In the moment when the mind is enlightened, the snake will be recognized as rope and fear and anxiety disappear in a flash, without therapy and without drugs. Light is sufficient for knowledge.

All who decide to start on the journey home - into the light - and try to unmask with discipline the delusion which the mind leads us to believe in, can have the experience that by the illumination of the darkness, what they doubted until now proves itself to be true. Everybody decides for himself when he will head on the journey. It is paradoxical that those who resist taking the first step on this journey are active as reporters of the journey and judge those who are on the journey for a long time. What would we think of someone who is criticizing a report of a journey and did himself never take one step out of his one-horse town?

The ignorant person is not able to reach higher states of consciousness, because the disharmonic state of his lower bodies will soon "get him back to reality," or, better stated, "get him back to his reality," because reality is subjective and corresponds to the individual state of evolution. This fact will bring science to desperate straits, as science pretends to be objective and pretends to explore reality and to search for generally valid laws. What to do when the generally valid reality does not exist?

Quantum physics, chaos research, transpersonal psychology and research of consciousness point towards the fact that every observation depends on the observer, meaning on his state of consciousness. This knowledge did not reduce the number of devotees of material science, because that takes from man the security of the supposed objectivity and burdens him with responsibility. Thus material science clings to delusive security and engages in head-in-the-sand policy. The psychologist belongs to the pioneers of the spiritual view and postulates the necessity of sciences oriented at the level of consciousness. Whoever believes matter to be the only reality should research by all means this transient construct. Whoever indeed knows that Spirit or energy is the basis of all matter and has priority, will deal with Spirit, the base, and with its manifestations, the effects.

The potter has to deal with the pot, the buyer of the pot not.
The creator has to deal with the substance, which is the base of his creation, the admirer of creation not.
The thinker has to deal with what produces thoughts, the receiver of the thoughts not.
The knower has to deal with what produces knowledge, the believer not.
One who is interested in the spheres of causes will not be satisfied to deal with the spheres of manifestation. One who is interested in man has to head off on the journey to the real man instead of dealing with a distorted picture.

"The higher spheres of consciousness are...the real causation, where ideas are conferred with a body and bodies are brought down to forms. Once you have succeeded in thrusting aside human consciousness, the fortune and the swing of feeling will truly support you, while you are proceeding on the 'wings of light' heavenwards." (Book of Life, p. 190*)

Michael Jackson talks about his understanding of this law as follows:

When all life is seen as divine, everyone grows wings.
Michael Jackson, Wings Without Me, Dancing the Dream

All life is divine; that means there is nothing which is separated from the divine, but the divine permeates everything, also the lower levels of manifestation, also matter. The separation between Spirit and matter is a concept and relates to different forms of expression, but not to the essence. There is no "i."

21. Messenger - Son - One

Michael Jackson conveys his message to the world through his songs, his music and his dance. Behind all pomp and splendor is hidden the knowledge about the power of stillness, music and the power of the One, who sends the music to the world. The effect is not dependent on the fact of the message comprehended with the mind, but on the consciousness carrying it. When it is soaked with love it operates on the deeper level of the soul and the heart, where man is touched immediately. The transformation of man starts by itself when he is profoundly touched.

Therefore there is no necessity for someone to present himself as a messenger as those do who are on a "ego trip"; it is sufficient to carry the message with all one's heart. "The messenger is never important. The message is that which makes alive," writes I, who says about his identity: "True IT does not sign itself, as this I does not denounce IT." (ICH, 1997, p. 3).

Michael Jackson knows that the message has an effect in itself and is able to contribute to the transformation of man:

That's why it's hard to take credit for the songs that I write, because I just always feel that it's done from above. I feel fortunate for being that instrument through which music flows. I'm just the source through which it comes. I can't take credit for it because it's god's work. He's just using me as the messenger.
Michael Jackson, Ebony, 1992

I believe performers should try to be strong as an example to their audiences.
Michael Jackson, Moonwalk, p. 281

"The reason to work should be to lead others on the path of duties by your example. Whatever the great one does the masses will imitate. His example is their incentive." Thus reads the commandment of Krishna to his pupil Arjuna in the Bhagavadgita, the millenia-old "Song of the Exalted."

In the history of mankind there are innumerable life streams, who were bestowed with the grace to realize their role as a messenger and to accept it. Sathya Sai Baba gives us in his Christmas speech in 1997 some information about the role of Jesus.

There were controversies in relation to Jesus. These differences in opinion were the cause for the martyrdom which he had to suffer. But Jesus was prepared to face each difficulty and each punishment. He considered compassion as the highest quality. First he declared himself to be "Messenger of God". Then he proclaimed "I am the Son of God". Finally he declared: "I and my father are One." You have to acknowledge this Oneness. You have to proclaim your Oneness and not your differences.

Sathya Sai Baba, Sanathana Sarathi, 01/1998

"Jesus taught us that the father is the principle by which humanity will reach the goal, that life has to be lived, that there is no secret in his deeds and teachings. The principle cannot change. It is possible to overlook it for an eternity, but in the moment in which one returns to it, one returns to the perfect state." (Spalding, Vol. 6, p. 59*)

The spiritual path is traditionally divided into three phases: purification, illumination, and unification (Tart, 1988). In the first phase man is purified from his egotism. His access to the higher bodies is still limited to a short flash. In the second phase man experiences a certain nearness and connectedness with his self, which can even continue for some time. In the third phase he realizes his identity, his Oneness with God. Then the only statement he can make about himself is: "I AM." All characteristics, all roles, all names and all forms have fallen away from him. They have to do nothing with his Self. He can use them like instruments, but the realized and illuminated one no longer falls into the trap of the delusion to identify himself with the instrument.

122

When man reaches the second phase he feels a deep connection with all living beings and a compassion which forces him to act and help when he is confronted with suffering and need. Buddha is said to have been the embodiment of compassion and to have been driven by the wish to show mankind the way out of suffering, confusion and delusion. Such life streams have reached a state of consciousness and a maturity which is difficult for ignorant people to understand. They are one in power, wisdom and love.

Michael Jackson attracts many people who feel his power, wisdom and love. They use it to deal with difficult life situations and heavy crises. Often they derive consolation and hope from his music and his words and their healing power saves them from self-destructive actions and even suicide. Countless life confessions were found in the 90's in the "Michael Jackson Internet Fan Club" (www.mjifc.com) - no longer available in 2015).
Michael is described as: "He is love."

Let's let talk one voice for many. Nancy Robinson writes on the occasion of the "Soul Train Awards" in 1993, when Michael received "Humanitarian Award": "His smile - total happiness which emanated from him. When his story will be told it will be a road map for us, when you enter the labyrinth of a dark, lonely, frightening world and find the way back to the bright sunshine without looking back. And the only price you get is that your soul is shining brighter than ever before. Is it possible that he shines brighter than in that night in the year 1993? I believe yes, **in God's eyes**, it must not be those of man. When he is still able to smile and reaches his hand and performs and embraces the world, we could perhaps make a little more effort to emphasize the positive in our own lives. That is my goal for 1993. To look at my little problems and needs as NOTHING...to look instead for the good in people, for the love, they would share and the hopes and dreams; then we can all help each other that it comes true."

Michael practices in his life for that for which man has incarnated on earth. He keeps to his vision of unity and follows his goal to channel the consciousness of man to oneness despite all resistance, animosity and disdain.

Today we stand together all around the world joined in a common purpose to remake the planet into a haven of joy, understanding and goodness. No one should have to suffer, especially our children. This time we must succeed. This is for the children of the world.
Michael Jackson, Super Bowl, 1993

After these words Michael Jackson starts on 31st of January his song "Heal the World" in Pasadena, California, during half time at the Super Bowl, which was broadcast live on TV with 133 million viewers worldwide. Those who did not have the chance to observe this event live can get an idea of the transforming power of the event on YouTube. Those who have already learned to see with the heart will certainly feel the tears of confidence, hope and compassion. (see also HIStory Video, Part 2, 1997).

22. Practiced Unity

There was a time when our ancestors lived with the knowledge that everything takes its course by united action, togetherness and faith in God to the benefit of everyone, and that man can easily reach his goals when he is devoted to God and allows Him to operate through him.

That is the path which the old ones followed. In those days there were no political parties or factions. All acted with one mind. That is the message of the Vedas: "Let's work together, let's have joy together, love each other and share our joy with everyone."
Sathya Sai Baba, Sanathana Sarathi, 11/1997

This appeal is as valid now as it was then. When will the call finally be heard? Only acting in the interest of all and sharing what we have on hand can bring the happiness which mankind is longing for.
Renunciation is the real secret of being happy. Everyone should share within his capabilities his income and his property and contribute to the welfare of others. It is the duty of the ones who are better off to go to the rescue of the unhappy ones.
Sathya Sai Baba, Sanathana Sarathi, 11/1997

Michael Jackson belongs to the richest people on this planet. His friends told us that even as a child he used the money he had on hand to buy presents and to give joy to other children and make them happy. By the grace of God, riches further flowed abundantly to him, so that he could give it away in the same way. He himself says that he accepts what he gets to give it away. Few people understand the importance of united action, thinking and feeling for the transformation of the world. The transforming power is derived from the source of love and the concentration of this love energy. When energy is dispersed its effectiveness is limited, as we see in the example of the sun's rays, which shine in all directions and give us light and warmth, but don't burn us. Only when the light rays are concentrated and focused, that is, directed to one point, is the resulting power sufficient to fan a flame or fire.

The same principle is valid for the power of thoughts or feelings which we emanate. When thoughts of love, healing and peace are sent to the world and to humanity, then these thoughts have the same power as the sun's rays. When they are concentrated and directed to one point, the power to light the fire of love, peace and harmony is then produced.

Albert Gaulden assures us: "I guarantee that the ego will descend into a death fight before your eyes and fall to the ground, as soon it will hear the angelic words - God, Truth, Love, Beauty, Peace, Balance and Harmony. The ego cannot stand the name of God."(Gaulden, 1997, p. 211)

Practiced unity can change the whole world - in short time. What decides the result is not the time which the power operates, but the intensity of the power. Intensity comes from one-pointedness of mind, by concentration of the mental and emotional energies on one issue, one goal. Man is not very successful in his various trials, because he does not understand the priority and force of mental power and tries instead to change on the level of physical manifestations. Michael Jackson puts his vision of tolerance and nonviolence in his songs.

And the whole world has to answer right now....We can change the world tomorrow, this could be a better place. If you don't like what I'm sayin' then won't you slap my face ....

Michael Jackson, Bad

The nonviolence which Michael is longing for is one of the five values which come to the fore in Sathya Sai Baba's teachings about formation of character. Nonviolence, âhimsa in Sanskrit, is the principle which Mahatma Gandhi followed to free India from British colonial rule. The knowledge about the power of these values should be taught and emphasized in our education.

"Vidyâ" means "acquisition of knowledge." In English it is called education. The term education comes from the Latin "edu-care," which means "to extricate." The idea thereby is to extricate what is already present latently.

Sathya Sai Baba, Sanathana Sarathi, 10/1997

126

Educare has two aspects, one which relates to the head and one which relates to the heart. The one which comes from the head is directed outward, and the one which comes from the heart is directed inward.
Sathya Sai Baba, Sanathana Sarathi, 12/1998

The acquisition of knowledge is nowadays only fostered in relation to earning one's livelihood. True education and formation are instead directed to the purpose and goal of human life. To perceive the relationship of man and cosmos, the spiritual aspects of life have to be understood and realized. Man proceeded on the earthly journey with the goal to realize his latent inward divinity and to manifest it outwardly. The measure of someone's credibility is the question: Does he practice what he is preaching? The world is full of preachers, but devoid of practitioners. Consistency of words, deeds and actions is the measure for the authenticity of a teaching.

Nonviolence in a narrower sense is not only the sacrifice of violence in dealing with conflicts, but not to cause harm to any being. Gandhi lived an exemplary model of the power of nonviolence: "Âhimsa, nonviolence, was for Gandhi the most noble expression of truth - or to be more accurate, the way to truth. Âhimsa and truth are so interrelated that it is practically impossible to disentangle and separate them. They are like the two sides of a coin, or rather a smooth, uncoined metal disc. Who can say which is the front side and which the back side? Nevertheless, âhimsa is the means and truth the purpose." (Easwaran, p. 120*)

The Sanskrit term âhimsa means "total lacking of any desire to kill." Âhimsa is one of the central values in Buddhism, Hinduism and Jainism. One who upholds this value will not kill animals and treats every life with awe. We were testimonies of his compassion for all living beings, when during a concert he discovered a small insect on stage and called security to take it away, so that nobody would step on it. When his bodyguard came to take it, Michael shouted: "Because I don't wanna, I don't wanna anybody step on this. Don't, don't kill it."
Michael Jackson, in a concert recording on You Tube

Do you know a more beautiful example of nonviolence?

"It is urgently required that we do everything possible to help bring about change. But we have to do it ourselves. Then it will start to reach others like a spiral and perhaps the world," is the persuasion of Phyllis Krystal due to her yearlong transformation work with people. (Krystal, 1995, p. XV*)

Whereas most people prefer to put the houses of others in order and to look for the splinter in the eye of the next ones while overlooking the beam in their own eyes, Michael Jackson knows that each one should start with himself: "I'm starting with the man in the mirror."
Michael Jackson, Man in the Mirror, HIStory album

In the HIStory album his message turns very impressive:
How many victims must there be, slaughtered in vain across the land? And how many struggles must there be before we choose to live the prophet's plan? How many people have to cry the song of pain and grief across the land before we stand to lend a healing hand?...Every child should sing together in harmony....All nations sing, let's harmonize all around the world.
Michael Jackson, HIStory, HIStory album

Modern information technology offers the possibility of aligning the consciousness of innumerable people to the same focus at the same time at the same place. If these people were not only passive spectators, but could be moved to participate actively to direct mentally elevating thoughts and healing feelings toward disease and suffering, they would create an indescribable mental power avalanche which could cause a change of consciousness and the healing of the world in short time. That would be the use of progress for the benefit of mankind and the planet and not an abuse - as so often been done in the past.

128

When people realize that all being is one and practice this unity, then the end of parties and factions, of groupings and fusions, of religions and worldviews could be sealed. When all people would only feel obliged to their higher conscience and would be faithful to themselves, then the conditions would be created that "His Will be Done." The One manifests His Will through our conscience.

Al Drucker gives us a hint as to how we can train our conscience. "How can we discern the voice of conscience from other voices? Where there are many voices you can call them 'conscious,' but not 'conscience.' Conscious is related to the lower self. It has to do with the mind. It contains many voices and differences. But conscience is always only one. It is unchangeable. You should learn to understand these different terms....The highest mind, the highest awareness, is pure consciousness. It is the one omnipresent reality. From it comes the conscience. From pure consciousness the conscience is originated. It is the voice of truth within us. Conscience is expression of the soul, the divine spark within us. It is the divinity which always is residing within us....That is the way which Jesus has shown you and it is also your way, Swami says." (Drucker, p. 28, 29*) To hear this conscience and to discern it from other voices, man has to clear and dissolve disharmonies and destructiveness in his emotional and mental bodies, turning into a useful instrument for the "plan of the prophet."

Michael Jackson asks:
How many victims must there be, slaughtered in vain across the land?
And how many struggles must there be, before we choose to live the prophet's plan?
Michael Jackson, HIStory, HIStory album

And in "Earth Song" he says:
What about the holy land? What about us?... Torn apart by creed.
What about us? What about the common man? What about us?

129

Can't we set him free? What about us?...What about children dying?
What about us?...What about Abraham? What about us?
Michael Jackson, Earth Song, HIStory album

What about the plan of the prophet? What about Abraham? Jesus'
mission was the abolition of the separation of races and classes and the
unification of mankind into a brotherhood. He taught us that the "seed of
Abraham" is only related to bodies, but man indeed is not a body, but the
"I." "Before Abraham was, was I" (Heindel, p. 364). This "I" is our
essence, which should be realized. Jesus was a teacher to the whole world
and he never wanted to establish a religion or a secession. That is the
product of ignorant followers, who called themselves Christians later on.
What arrogance and delusion to believe that the embodiment of love, who
walked on earth under the name of Jesus, has come to save some people
and condemn others, to include some people in his love and exclude
others! Such insane ideas can only be conceived by the "lying, fraudulent,
thievish and misidentified ego with all his false promises" (Gaulden, p.
211*).

Man is one without a second. The universe is one without a second.
Everything which exists is one without a second and everything which
does not exist is one without a second. More and more people are
maturing and awakening to this knowledge. Man is beginning to
understand and to accept that he is not what his thoughts try to persuade
on him, but that he is a perfect being, who only has identified himself
erroneously with a distorted picture of himself. Slowly he is getting ready
to accept his inheritance as a king instead of living the illusion of a beggar.
Michael Jackson is bearing for the just cause hostility, defamation, injury,
slander and lies. He is haunted and chased by the mob, by the ignorant
press and the media, even by many fans, who are on the chase for energy
and idols. They don't understand that unity cannot be found on the level
of physical bodies, but only on the level of the "I," where "I" and "You"
are one, and this That and He is I.

Sathya Sai Baba states the reason for persecution:

Some people cannot tolerate the fame of others, some are filled with the poison of envy; some are of demonic nature and cannot tolerate holiness and divinity. Some are blinded by disappointment and try to blame God. Such people will make defaming speeches.
Sathya Sai Baba Speaks, Vol. 8, Chap. 32*

As it is impossible for "normal" adults with their programmed brains, their "prejudices, criticisms, assignment of guilt, greed, self-relatedness and other perversions of the critical mind" (Gaulden, p. 188) to accept people who are different, Michael Jackson has withdrawn from most of these people and turned to spend time with children.

23. Guilt - Innocence

Michael Jackson dedicates twelve of the poems and stories in "Dancing the Dream" to the children: When Babies Smile - Children of the World - The Boy and the Pillow - Children - Innocence - Ryan White - On the Children of the World - Wise Little Child - A Child is a Song - Child of Innocence - Magical Child, Part 1 - Magical Child, Part 2. These not only refer to the child in the biological phase of childhood, but also to the aspect of the "inner child," the "magical child" in all of us. This is the wiser, more caring and creative part compared to the adult, which is suppressed and repressed by society and our educational system. It is the part which Jesus related to: "Truly I tell you, unless you change and become like little children, you will never enter the kingdom of heaven. Therefore, whoever takes the lowly position of this child is the greatest in the kingdom of heaven." (Matthew 18: 3-4)

That's what I love about being with kids. They notice everything. They aren't jaded. They get excited by things we've forgotten to get excited about any more. They are so natural too, so unself-conscious. I love being around them.... They energize me-just being around them. They look at everything with such fresh eyes, such open minds. That's part of what makes kids so creative. They don't worry about the rules. The picture doesn't have to be in the center of the piece of paper. They sky doesn't have to be blue. They are accepting of people too. The only demand they make is to be treated fairly-and to be loved. I think, that's what we all want.

I would like to think that I'm an inspiration for the children I meet. I want kids to like my music. Their approval means more to me than anyone else's.

Michael Jackson, Moonwalk, p. 274, 275

After Michael Jackson's performance at "Wetten Dass" in November 1997 the then German chancellor Gerhard Schröder stated: "Now I understand his fans, he has something touching" (Ebmeier, p. 220*). And Michael's brother Jermaine says: "Would more of us have stayed so childlike as he, the world would be in a better state" (Ebmeier, p. 239*). Michael Jackson is searching for the truth, with which children are still connected. In two poems he talks about "Innocence":

Yet there is a deep truth in innocence. A baby looks in his mother's eyes, and all he sees is love. As innocence fades away, more complicated things take its place.
Michael Jackson, Innocence, Dancing the Dream

Michael Jackson dedicates another poem to innocence:

Child of innocence, I miss your sunny days...

Child of innocence, return to me now...

Child of innocence...

Come fly with me far and above,

Over the mountains in the land of love...

Child of innocence, messenger of joy

You've touched my heart...

My soul is ablaze with a flagrant fire

To change this world is my deepest desire.
Michael Jackson, Child of Innocence, Dancing the Dream

Elizabeth Taylor describes her friend: "I think Michael Jackson appeals to the child in all of us, and I think he has the quality of innocence that we would all like to obtain or to have kept."
(Dancing the Dream, Introduction)

Mencius, a Confucian philosopher, is cited as follows: "A great man is one who has kept his childlike heart" (Süddeutsche Zeitung, 28th Feb. 1998). In April 1973 Sathya Sai Baba said:

I like young and innocent souls, I don't allow that they are blamed.
Sathya Sai Baba Speaks, Vol. 8, chap. 44*

Because I find in animals the same thing I find so wonderful in children. That purity, that honesty, where they don't judge you. They just want to be your friend.... To be as pure as children, and to make yourself as innocent and to see the world through eyes of wonderment and the whole magical quality of it all and I love that.

Michael Jackson, Oprah Winfrey Interview, 1993

Who wonders why Michael Jackson has children as friends.
The children of the world, for their innocence, their simplicity, and their love. It's the same kind of innocence that I find in animals. They just want you for your love and I love that.

Michael Jackson, Simulchat, 17th Aug. 1995 (www.allmichaeljackson.com)

When Louis Armstrong in his legendary song "Wonderful World" praises the wonders of the world, he then expresses what everyone who wears glasses of innocence is feeling: this world is a composition of beauty and magic. In contrast the so-called monkey mind is seeing a world of greed and hate, so we are unable to see the world without filters and with the glasses of innocence - as it really is. Michael Jackson gives to his son Prince the following message to take with him on his life journey:

Not the stars, not the most distant solar systems, not the million different types of animal life, but the child is the greatest in God's creation.

Michael Jackson, Life, December 1997, p. 96

Michael describes the experience of witnessing his son's birth as:
...it is an incredibly joyful experience....I am in bliss 24 hours a day.
There is no miracle in life that compares with watching your son come
into the world....I couldn't believe the miracle I had witnessed. It was
unbelievable!
Michael Jackson, OK magazine, 4th April 1997

Michael Jackson raises our awareness of the danger of mind
conditioning and the undone chance of exhausting and enhancing the
potential in humans:
I love children, as you can see. And babies....Well there's a certain
sense that animals and children have that gives me a certain creative
juice, a certain force that later on in adulthood is kind of lost because
of the conditioning that happens in the world. A great poet said
once: "When I see children I see that God has not yet given up on
man." A poet from India said that, and his name is Tagore. The
innocence of children represents to me the source of infinite
creativity. That is the potential of every human being. But by the
time you are an adult, you're conditioned, you're so conditioned by
the things about you and it goes.
Michael Jackson, Ebony, May 1992

Like the old Indian proverb says, do not judge a man until you've
walked two moons in his moccasins.... I worry about the children, all my
children all over the world, I live for them....But still I must achieve. I
must seek truth in all things. I must endure for the power I was sent
forth, for the world for the children.
Michael Jackson, Open Letter to his Critics, People, 12th October 1987

For many years Michael Jackson wore an armband on the right upper arm in different colors at various events and on stage. He declared and explained that he will wear this sign of grief as long as there are still children in the world who suffer. What boundless compassion! Michael Jackson's service to the world is not only related to the improvement of physical life conditions and the relief of emotional suffering, but is also based on the idea and vision of oneness, on the wish to unite the whole of humanity. This is truly the vision of "brotherhood of man and fatherhood of God," as it was called by Sathya Sai Baba.

Michael Jackson's specialty is the hymn. He puts in hymns the voice of his soul in the most intense way. They are the medium and way to reach and touch the spiritual hearts of his listeners. These hymns don't only touch the heart of children, but all those whose heart is still touchable, when it is not yet stoned - he reaches all those in the state of innocence, because they don't know or pay attention to the guilt of the ego, but know about their original divine nature.

The ego uses guilt in the following way: "The purpose of the ego is fear, because only those filled with fear can be egotistic....That which is really blessed is unable to raise fear, but has to raise joy. Thus it is immune against the ego, because his peace cannot be attacked....Guilt is always disturbing....Everything which creates fear creates separation, because it obeys the law of separation. When the ego is the symbol of separation, so it is also the symbol of guilt." (Course in Miracles, Chapter 5, V.*)

I turn to them (children) for new life, for new music. Two brown eyes look at me so deeply, so innocently, and inside I murmur, "This child is a song." It is so true and direct an experience that instantly I realize again, "I am a song also." I am back to myself once more.
Michael Jackson, A Child is a Song, Dancing the Dream

"Let the little children come to me and do not hinder them, for the kingdom of God belongs to such as these." (Mark 10:14) This was Jesus' promise to all those who know their father and accept their childship to God. Michael Jackson believes in this power and spirit of innocence:

Children of the world, we'll do it...we'll swing the tide of time and do it...Children of the world, we'll do it...With song and dance and innocent bliss...we'll do it.
Michael Jackson, Children of the World, Dancing the Dream

    The child in us is the part which sees with the heart and did not separate from primal completeness. To this child Michael Jackson has dedicated his album HIStory:

"With these words, I lovingly dedicate this album of my music to all the children of the world: Let us dream of a tomorrow where our children are nurtured, and protected and nourished. Let us dream of peace and harmony and laughter. Let us dream of joy and ecstasy.
Let us dream of dancing the cosmic dance. Let us renew again those dreams of promise we once made before, where we can hold our heads high and stretch our arms toward perfection.
Let us dream of a tomorrow, where we can truly love from the soul and know love as the ultimate truth in the heart of all creation."
Michael Jackson, HIStory album, cover (http://aln2.albumlinernotes.com/HIStory_-_Book_One.html)

24. Image

One who knows the love that never interferes has found the second bird. Sathya Sai Baba talks about it: *The individual, jivin in Sanskrit, and the universal, îshvara in Sanskrit, are two birds which are sitting on the same tree, the human body. The individual acts and suffers the consequences of his acting. The universal sits still, as spectator of the other bird. When the individual looks at the universal and realizes that it is nothing other than his image, then he escapes sorrow and suffering....Then the realization of the self, atman in Sanskrit, is reached.*
Sathya Sai Baba, Upanishad Vahini, p. 28*

The term "image" is also found in the history of creation in the Christian bible. "Then God said: 'Let us make mankind in our image, in our likeness....So God created mankind in his own image, in the image of God he created them....And it was so. God saw all he had made, and it was very good...the sixth day. *(Genesis 1:26,27,30, 31)* On the sixth day of creation man appears on earth as the image of God. Does man live this function as an image? Has mankind already reached the sixth day of creation? Does man really equal God? Sathya Sai Baba teaches us that the way to it is only possible with love.

Love is expansion, inclusion and reciprocity. The individual has to be universalized, expand as long as it embodies the whole creation.
Sathya Sai Baba, Sanathana Sarathi, 8/1997*

Creation is not an act finished within six days of our calendar, but is an ongoing process which is not yet completed and takes place on an individual level as well as on a collective level. Eastern traditions of wisdom teach that everything is always expanding, that expansion is a characteristic of everything, starting with our material universe to the universe of consciousness.

At the beginning of this century also, academic science has discovered this fact. It is indeed so frightening and unimaginable for "plains theorists" that many refuse to acknowledge it. Instead to dive deep they are concentrating on the faults of those who have access to deeper realms unknown to those who are staying at the shallow shores. Einstein himself called the discovery and assumption of an antigravity the biggest blunder of his life. This insight blew his mind and his power of imagination. It did not fit in his worldview, although he was much more comprehensive than most of his contemporaries. Even such a genius as Einstein was tempted to use the bed of Procrustes. Sathya Sai Baba calls this the reason for the misery of the world state.

The world is drifting into the ruin due to myriads of problems. What is the healer? A radical change in the thinking of man has to occur. Men should realize their innate divinity.
Sathya Sai Baba, Sanathana Sarathis 11/1997*

Nearly one century after its discovery, empirical science is behaving as if the results of the theory of relativity and quantum physics respectively have never existed and were only valid for the subatomic level without relevance for the behavior and consciousness of man. A recent study which was published in the magazine "Science" doubts the theory of the Big Bang and has proven the effect of antigravity, by which the cosmos is expanding with increasing velocity (Süddeutsche Zeitung, 28th Feb. 1998).

The natural sciences are only dealing with a tiny realm of reality and cannot understand the permanent process of evolution and miss the essence of the universe and creation. The ancient hermetic principle of the wise Hermes Trismegistos which says, "As above, so below," indicated the way thousands years ago how to find real knowledge and search the truth. But as long as the sciences are following a wrong track they will continue to go round in circles.

Stephen Hawkings, one of the masterminds of modern physics, who is searching for the world formula, believed in 1992 that before the end of the century a unified theory of physics and behavior would be found, able to explain the background of all things (Hawkings, 1992). Indeed this world formula has to consider that the individual, the particular, is nothing other than the appearance of the universal, its reflection, the image of the universal. As above, so below!

The laws of the macrocosm are the same that govern the microcosm, the atom. The powers that hold together the cosmos are the same that hold together people in communities, groups, families, etc. Sathya Sai Baba declares:

The mantra OM contains the powers of shiva and shakti. These two powers, shiva and shakti, correspond to that which the scientists call electron and proton, the two parts of the atom. The proton forms the core of the atom. The electron moves with high velocity around the proton. The Veda described this phenomenon differently. It declared that shiva and shakti are inseparably connected. This corresponds to the relation of proton and electron. Prior to proton and electron there exists a particle which is known as a neutron. This corresponds to what the Veda called "sat." "Sat" means darkness. From this darkness is born the light.
Sathya Sai Baba, Sanathana Sarathi, 04/1997*

The so-called enlightened people cannot imagine that the knowledge about atoms and their essence was already written down 5000 years ago in the Vedas, the oldest scriptures of Indian literature. The language is different from ours, but the meaning is the same.

Finally there is only one power to which all other powers can be reduced and which holds together everything, be it protons and electrons, shiva and shakti, or man and woman - this attracting and binding power is love. It is the tendency to melt that which is innate in everything which exists, which is inherent in every phenomenon, occurrence and manifestation. It is called negentropy in physics, and known as the level of disorder and chaos. In reality everything which is manifested is aiming to reach this state, the state of dissolution of forms, the merging into the formless, which is called the "void" or "nirvana" in Buddhism, which man will enter at the end of his life cycle. It is the state of formless energy, of light, the state which is known as liberation, salvation or awakening.

Sathya Sai Baba confirms: *The final reality is the energy of the atom. Everything which is perceived or observed in the manifest cosmos is the*

*combination of atoms. The five basic elements are made of atoms. The food you
ingest, the water you drink, the air you inhale, the sound you hear, are all
different form of expression of atoms. The cosmos is made of atoms.*
Sathya Sai Baba, Sanathana Sarathi, 01/1996*

Man is the image of God. An image is a copy of an original with the
same characteristics as the original. Bob Jones, CEO of Michael Jackson's
enterprise, MJJ Productions, has said about Michael: "He is a composite
of the image that nature desires for every individual to attain."
(C. Mecca, The essence).

In the nineties I had an experience which provided me with the
understanding and the knowledge of the essence of nature in an instant
like a flash. I was attending a workshop on "holotropic breathing" (Grof,
1988). By the method of hyperventilation a process is initiated which
brings experiences and information from the subconscious level into
consciousness. Most of the upcoming information is that of traumatic
experiences from childhood or sometimes even from earlier lives, which
by this method - accompanied by music and with the support of a
psychotherapist - will be acknowledged, solved and integrated. The
process proceeds by itself, without control of the mind, and usually will
last five to six hours. The breathing person is lying on a mat and is
supervised by a sitter. My experience was as follows:
I only perceive darkness and "nothing." After some time I understand
that I have to create the universe if something besides "nothing" shall
exist. I breathe more forcefully so that light originates. FIAT LUX - let
there be light. It is a very exhausting process. Minerals originate - the first
day of creation.

I pause and relax for a short time. Everything is good. Then I continue
to breathe intensely so that creation can progress. Much power is needed.
Plants originate by inhaling and exhaling. Then I see the first flower and I
am enchanted by its beauty and magnificence. I admire the creation - the
second day.

141

I continue breathing; there follow animals. I see a libeller - the third day of creation.

I realize that I am the creator. When I stop breathing everything will vanish; thus I have to continue to breathe. It is my will to continue. I recognize that there is no necessity for the universe to originate, but only due to my will. I want to create diversity so that I can love myself. I find everything very good, approve it, continue to breathe. I create men facing their magnificence. I am in a state of pure bliss.

In between comes the thought that it is crazy that I myself have to create the whole universe. Why is there nobody to help me? I ask my inner master for help. His answer is: "There is no one separate from you to help because there is only you."
Slowly the knowledge dawns of what is the meaning of this answer. There is only I. I am overwhelmed by joy and thankfulness. The fourth day of creation is completed.

I feel peace, highest peace, prashanti in Sanskrit. I see colors that can only be described as heavenly, because the most beautiful colors of the rainbow cannot match them. They are spinning around, tiny countless energy particles. I hear choirs of angels - no earthly music - which rejoice and praise the magnificence of being. There is only I and my work of creation.
I continue to breathe, fifth day of creation.

To complete the next day everyone has to realize that they are I. Only then can creation step into the sixth day and be completed. Everyone has to realize that there is only ONE and not two or many, that there is only one LOVE and nothing else. On the seventh day everything will then relax in this love, unmovable, in peace and bliss.

I feel that a love for all which exists and everyone is flowing through me. This state cannot be describes in words. I abide in this state for a long while, without thoughts, without emotions...

When i then open my eyes - i have no idea how long this whole process was going on - the world does not look like before anymore, and ever since then it has not returned again to its former state.

I talk about my experience to the female sitter who has accompanied and supervised me for the last six hours. She was not surprised about my experience, but told me that she had seen that there was a "birth by heart" under way.

Creation is a birth by heart. i am overwhelmed by the depth of my feelings and the depth of our connection. i understand that truth is only hearable in the depth of silence and cannot be seen with the outer eyes, but only with the heart.

i know that I have created the cosmos and that creation is not yet completed. The fifth day of creation will be finished when all people have understood that they are "I". Ken Wilber says it as follows: "And while you are now reading this book try to remember: remember the great event when you exhaled and created this whole cosmos" (Wilber, 1998, p. 57*). What does that mean? The "i" with which we are identifying is not our real identity, but I AM.

You have to realize that the "i" is only an instrument of the Lord. Like this fan you too are an instrument of the Lord. Does this fan turn around with its own power or is it driven by electricity?...God is the electricity; you are only the instrument.
*Sathya Sai Baba, cit. in Hislop, p. 13**

The way people are using the word "i" is the biggest maneuver of delusion you can imagine. The ego is "an impostor who claims to be I. Who keeps me from living my true life? Who frightens me, who holds me little, who does not want me to grow, who does not want me to awake?" (Fox, 1998, p. 97*). The only purpose of the ego is to prevent us from knowing ourselves, meaning that we know God. It uses the same name which is used for the nameless and formless I. "FATHER today I awake with miracles which correct my perception of all things....I want to forget all things besides YOUR LOVE....And I want to find the peace which

YOU created for YOUR son, and I want forget all the stupid toys I desire, while I behold YOUR glory and my own," says "A Course in Miracles" (lecture 346).

The "i" which identifies itself with the body turns into the ego. The ego wears a form wherever it goes. But the formless "I," which is not identified with the body, is the atman. The formless atman has no characteristics. People nowadays only experience the "i" which is identified with the body. They cannot imagine an "I" without a body. But if instead the body is treated as the base and the sight is turned inward, the atman can be experienced in due time. That is called "direct perception of the Self." It means to follow the "I" to its source.
Sathya Sai Baba, Sanathana Sarathi, 11/1997

25. Insight - In-Sight - One Sight

The direction of our sight has to be reversed. Instead of outwardly it has to be directed inwardly. Instead of delighting at the out-sight, joy has to originate from in-sight; only then will we turn insightful. When we are insightful and find One sight due to inward sight, we have found the key for the next step of evolution. In the age of enlightenment, humanity was led in the wrong direction for a long time. Even when the outward sight, the outlook, and the surface are explored thoroughly, they remain superficial and remain on the outer side. Even when everyone believes that the view outside is everything in life, the truth will not change. Truth will not turn untrue because it is denied or unknown. And untruth does not become truth when it is propagated. Man possesses the ability of discrimination to discern between holy and canting things.

Sathya Sai Baba reminds us: *Man who stands with his back to the sun will step on his own shadow. Only when he returns he can leave his shadow behind him.*
Sathya Sai Baba, Sanathana Sarathi, 11/1997*

Most people prefer to escape their shadow instead of confronting it. Michael Jackson tells us how he is dealing with the shadow:

Many a time I tried to break this shadow following me I could not shake. Many a time...I peered behind to see its trace. I could not lose it in any place.

It was only when I broke all ties...I suddenly stared in your fiery eyes. All at once I found my goal. The elusive shadow was my soul.
Michael Jackson, The elusive shadow, Dancing the Dream

And Sathya Sai Baba says:
The journey has to be directed to the self inside and away from the outer world...Thus you see the Divine in everything instead of looking at nature as a

145

physical phenomenon. When you look at the outer world as manifestation of God, you will not notice the phenomenal aspect of nature. Look at nature as a manifestation of God.
Sathya Sai Baba, Sanathana Sarathi, 11/1997

Nature is called "prakriti" in Sanskrit; it is the manifested aspect of the unmanifested energy, the visible aspect of the invisible, the hearable aspect of the unhearable. As we cannot look directly into the sun, as we would be blinded by its light, but look at it as a reflection in the water, so nature is a reflection of what we cannot perceive directly, because it is formless, nameless and attributeless - the mirror of the essence, the core, the original nature, named "purusha" in Sanskrit. Even when talking about two aspects - "prakriti" and "purusha" - the two are not separated, but image and archetype, nature and Spirit, the two birds, Michael is talking about - One. Whoever only looks at the phenomenon easily forgets that nothing can exist without a cause. He believes the fata morgana to be real. He is sleeping and continues dreaming the century-old dream of humanity. Why should we deny him some more years of deep slumber?

26. I - You - We

First "i", then "you." "I" plus "you" is "we." Then comes "we" plus "he" and then only "He....First "i," then "you." "I" is life. "You" is the world. "I" plus "you" is "we" - creation. "We" plus "he" is God. Then only "He."
Sathya Sais Baba, cit. in Hislop, 1994, p. 12*

From "i" to "He," from the undifferentiated ego to the nameless. On this journey man crosses the level of "we," as Michael Jackson says:

The truth is that you and I would have given up long ago, but We won't let us. It is too wise. "Look into your hearts," it says. "What do you see? Not you and I, but only We."
Michael Jackson, I You We, Dancing the Dream

Jack Hislop cites Sathya Sai Baba:
"We" plus "he" is God. Then only "He." That is the love, the lover and the beloved. When everything is one, bliss arises.
Sathya Sai Baba, cit. in Hislop, 1994, p. 13*

I become the lover and the beloved....

The creator and creation merge into one wholeness of joy.
Michael Jackson, The Dance, Dancing the Dream, / Cover Dangerous-Album

These words of Michael Jackson witness how deeply his experience is reaching, and that in reality there are no opposites. The mystic Master Eckehart said: "Man is born twice. Once into the world and once out of the world." That is the realization of the "second bird." The awakened is living in the world, but he is not of this world. People whose consciousness is residing on the deeper levels are not able to understand those on the higher levels. The big mistake of the know-it-all is the belief that all who are staying in a human body are living on the same evolutionary level of the consciousness ladder. Who nowadays is able to understand Buddha or Jesus or Mohamed or Sathya Sai Baba? Who really understands "common" people like Einstein or Gandhi or Mother Teresa or Michael Jackson or Jane Doe?

Understanding requires the realization of the "second bird." One who has realized the "second bird" knows that there is only "One bird." That the second bird is the reflection, the image, of the first. Then the search for the self is ended, because i found "I."

The realization of the self is the condition for the realization of God. The temple of Apollo already invited us to start with this task. After entering the temple and looking back, one could see the letter "epsilon" above the entrance, which was pronounced "you are." Only one who realizes himself is allowed to say "you are" to another one. Only self-realization leads to the realization of the other one, to the realization that the other is my Self.

Modern society has twisted this ancient wisdom. We believe that we know others when we have seen their body and know their name. We arrogate to be able to judge and evaluate them. But these judges are not able to answer the question. "Who am I?" They arrogate to know who the other is without knowing who they themselves are. "Let he who is without sin cast the first stone," is Jesus' requirement. The law of balance, karma in Sanskrit, says that every action is followed by an aligned reaction. Everything returns to the originator like a boomerang. Indeed the law of cause and effect does not determine which form the reaction will take. Thus the stone throwers don't realize that the stones they find on their way are the stones they have thrown there before. The law of seed and harvest is relentless, reliable, impersonal and absolutely just. We are living in the illusion of being victims and strokes of fate, because we don't know all links of the chain of cause and effect, but only a part of the whole puzzle of billions of particles. When somebody says, "would I be blind..." and is born blind in his next life, why should we have pity? It was his will. He may need help and compassion bearing his self-created cross, but not regret and pity. He is not a poor innocent victim, but a victim of his own deeds and desires. When we emanate hate, it will catch up to us sometime. When we hate foreigners, we may be born in a foreign country in our next life and experience firsthand all the hate we have emanated in this life.

148

There is sufficient proof for the law of balance, which we will not elaborate in this book (Cayce 1991).

Ramana Maharshi, who left the earthly plane in the year 1950, one of the great masters and holy men of modern times, recommended to his followers to advance tirelessly their self-exploration with the question: "Who am I?" At age 17, he had a spontaneous experience of the "I," which reversed the direction of his life completely. "The fear of death vanished completely and forever. This certainty of the immediate presence of the SELF, which is independent of the body, has never left me since." (Schmidt, p. 379*)

Even as a child, Michael Jackson was fascinated by the question: I am especially fond of the scene (in the Wiz) where Diana (Ross) asks "What am I afraid of? Don't know what i am made of..." because I've felt that way many times, even during the good moments of my life.
Michael Jackson, Moonwalk, p. 138, 140

Michael is accompanied by these questions throughout his life: Who I am? Who are you? Where did we come from? Where are we going? What's it all about? Do you have the answers?
Michael Jackson, Are you listening? Dancing the Dream

Sathya Sai Baba tells us about Ramana Maharshi: *Ramana Maharshi said always to his pupils who came to him: "Know yourself" does not mean to know facts about your body, your mind or your senses. You have to find the answer to the question: "Who am I?". The body, the senses, the mind and intellect are all your instruments. You are the master. Master the mind and be the master. For a human being atman is the master. It is the power of atman which enables the senses to fulfill its different functions like hearing, seeing, etc. You have therefore to realize that you are the atman and not the body.*
Sathya Sai Baba, Sanathana Sarathi, 11/1997*

Practicing this method, every answer to the question, "Who am I," is canvassed thoroughly and it is examined if one is no longer "I," when an attribute does not apply to the body and mind. Thus one by one everything which is not "I" is excluded until one has reached the Self. *Only the spiritual teacher can open the inner eye and purify the inner instruments of intuition. He prompts you to ask yourself: "Am I this body or is this body only a vehicle which I am using?" and to discover the answer. "I am not this body, I am the observer, the witness, the watcher." Then the question follows, if the I is real: "Who am I then?" And the answer lights up in pure consciousness. "I am He; I am a spark of this Magnificence; I am God".*
Sathya Sai Baba Speaks, Vol. 8*

The Self, the I, cannot be described with words: "The TAO that can be spoken is not the eternal TAO. The name which can be named is not the eternal Name", thus Laotse starts in the Tao te Ching (www.taoism.net).

"I say to you Bleris, the people in this world will forget for so long until they don't even know themselves. Because they have forgotten where they come from and where they are going," says Merlin (Kübler, p.92*). Magician and seer Merlin prompts Bleris to write down the things that are happening, so that they will someday give someone notions to remember again. What is written down cannot effect the remembering, but it can motivate someone to search for healing from the state of amnesia.

27. It is a Scream

In the parable of seven days of creation is hidden a deep secret. The number seven is a symbol which we find in all cultures, all religions and many myths. Michael Jackson also uses it in his lyrics and films. The video "Scream" has seven parts, which illustrate the cycle of creation and at the same time deplore the misery of the world: 1. GRAvitation, 2. HABITation, 3. GALLery, 4. MEDium, 5. mEDITation, 6. PRESERVation and 7. reCREATion.

The film leads the viewer in time lapse through this cycle. A space ship is flying in the universe. Inside an automat with stress capsules. Gravity pulls us down to the dense matter and is chaining us to the earth, which produces stress. Michael with headphones in a hatch, arms crossed before his chest. A view on the space ship which is swallowed by a ball of light. Michael shuts his ears and appears in the hatch, his face contorted with pain. Janet too. Both ascend the walls weightlessly inside the ship, alternating individually and together in a frantic aggressive dance. On the screen appears the face of a screaming anime child. Michael smashes a guitar on the ground. Then follow seven scenes where close shots and totals are constantly changing.

1.GRAvity: Michael is floating in space, whereby he seems to "drill" his inculpating forefinger in the face of the viewer, is crossing himself, bumping into others.

Tired of injustice....the whole system sucks.

Michael Jackson, Scream

Face to face, Michael and Janet are snarling at each other, screaming, floating in space, with defensive hand gestures. Abruptly Michael protects Janet in his arms. Again change to aggression, whereby Janet is bumping the sole of her foot into the face of the viewer. Screaming child on the screen. Michael again smashes his guitar.

2. HABITation: tenement, "habit" means by custom. Wild dance, Janet goes up the wall.

You tell me I'm wrong, then you better prove you're right.

Michael Jackson, Scream

3. GALLery: the highest gallery in the theatre is "the gods." Gall means bitterness. In German we say: "mir kommt die Galle hoch" (my blood was up). A door is leading to a hallway; Michael sitting in a futuristic chair with a remote control in his hands. He projects a face on the screen which morphs to a network. Janet projects a rock which morphs into a Buddha and then a Christian statue. Michael morphs the network into a framed portrait with an apple face.

Stop pressurin' me, stop pressurin' me, stop pressurin' me, make me wanna scream.

Michael Jackson, Scream

The spaceship departs.

4. MEDium: mass media, medium also means "channel for higher intuition" or "middle" or "mediocrity" in German. Michael and Janet are sitting in a cinema playing computer games; a ball is ping-ponged.

Tired of you telling me the story your way...keep changin' the rules.

Michael Jackson, Scream

Both are fighting for the joystick, Janet with unkempt hair, tiny bikini and long open coat behind a table, aggressive, screaming and provocative. Weightless dancing and wildly screaming. The space ship is approximating the earth, weightless dancing, it departs. A door opens, Janet appears wild.

5. mEDITation: is formed from the yin-yang symbol. In between wild dance, individually and collectively. Michael appears in the meditation room in lotus position.

Oh father, please have mercy, 'cause I just can't take it.

Michael Jackson, Scream

6. OBSERVation: Watching. Janet in the men's restroom. Both are dancing wildly and aggressively; Janet is nearly scratching out the eyes of the spectator. A newsreader appears on the screen.

Oh my God can't believe what I saw as I turned on the TV this evening.

Newsman: A man has been brutally beaten to death by police. After being wrongfully identified as a robbery suspect. The man was an eighteen-year-old black male.

Michael Jackson, Scream

Switch to the meditation room. Michael in lotus position, his head is surrounded by an aureole of light. In the meditation room the glass roof bursts due to Michael's screams. Switch: Both are dropping to the floor on their knees, dancing. The earth is visible in the burst round glass roof as shattered glass is still floating from the ceiling. Michael and Janet are dancing, crossing themselves. On the screen Michael appears with earphones. Janet is dancing in front; then they change positions. Janet appears with earphones; Michael is dancing in front. Change to the space ship in the universe. Michael aiming with a tennis racket at nine vases. Switch to the space ship in the universe. A guitar is floating in space.

7. reCREATion: means leisure time or new creation. Michael is wearing a T-shirt with the number seven, smashes a vase. In between Janet and Michael with ear phones, two vases are smashed. Wild dancing at the ceiling. The newsman is screaming and is tearing his hair like Janet.

I think I might go insane. With such confusion don't it make you wanna scream?

Michael Jackson, Scream

Clouds of smoke on the screen, the guitar is thrown away, on the screen a screaming cartoon character. Michael is on his knees in front of the screen. The word "Scream" in transparent letters is crumbling. Janet screaming, both catch the other in their arms and Michael's screaming head defamiliarizes.

He himself comments on the film "Scream":

Sometimes the only thing you can do is scream. Don't you ever feel like this? You just want to let everything out. People should listen and then decide for themselves.

Michael Jackson, www.mjifc.com* (Site no longer available).

We can hear the song, see the video and then get back to business as usual or we can hear it and listen to it. Hearing is passive doing; listening is active doing. Those who have liberated themselves from the stranglehold of the plains and are ready to ascend to the heights or descend into the depths can catch a glimpse of what Michael Jackson wants to express with the Sevenness. "Whoever has ears, let them hear" (Matthew 11:15, 13:43) say the Gospels. Taraborrelli writes that Michael told him that the number seven has always had a mystical significance for him and is very important for him. The seven phases in "Scream" are symbolic of the history of creation.

1. The power of gravitation which affects matter binds man, who identifies himself as with matter and his physical body. On earth he is confronted with disharmony, aggression and injustice. "Gravity" also means seriousness and indicates the seriousness of the actual state.

2. Earth turns into the home of man, where he is tied by his habits, so there's nothing left to do but climb the walls. .

3. On the gallery man is in the public's mercy as if living in a fishbowl. Thus he serves as projection surface; the result is anger and bitterness. The projection imposes something onto the things which does not really belong to them. The projector is man who does not see things how they are, but how he wants them to be - due to selective perception.

4. Projections are spread by the media. The ball is ping-ponged. Aggression is followed by defense and again aggression. Back and forth, joy and pain, fortune and misfortune, up and down, fight and reconciliation, diction and contradiction. All these are moves in the balance game of dual life, in a world of opposites fighting for domination. There is no other purpose than to create victor and vanquished, and to

154

determine on which side the balance will move upward or downward. As the balance is not balanced, the whole game will start again and again. "As long as you perceive the body as your reality, so long will you perceive yourself as lonely and deprived. Deprivation nourishes aggression as there is the conviction that aggression is justified" (Course in Miracles Chapter 15, XI, 5, 1, 7*).

5. By meditation the waves will calm down for a while. Man remembers his second half, a chance for unity of yin and yang. These are not opposites but the two sides of a coin, different aspects of the same thing. The symbol of yin-yang is a symmetrical structure of the dark yin and the bright yang, which is not static but dynamic, which is indicated by the dark point in the bright and the bright point in the dark. In every pole the other pole is latently included. Existence is a constant change between these poles, like the up and down of waves in the ocean. "The Tao produced One, the One produced Two, Two produced Three, Three produced All things. All things leave behind them the Obscurity and go forward to embrace the Brightness, while they are harmonized by the Breath of Vacancy" (Tao te Ching, 42, www.sacred-texts.com).

The Chinese discovered more than 2500 years ago a system of cosmic archetypes, which is known as "I Ching" or "The Book of Changes." It contains in encoded form all information about the cosmos - microcosm and macrocosm - man and the universe. Due to its deep wisdom of life the I Ching is also used as an oracle. "In this book is constructed a system of parables for the whole world," Hermann Hesse wrote. The I Ching is composed of 64 hexagrams, all possible combinations of yin and yang. These resemble the structure of the human DNA, the genetic code. Its significance is revealed during deep contemplation and not accessible to the thinking mind. "Whoever knows does not talk, whoever talks does not know" says the Tao philosopher Chuang-tzu.

6. Then follows the phase of observation, consideration, where all habits are discarded and awareness is growing. Things are not judged in accordance with their outer appearance, but conceived with the inner eye. In meditation all patterns are figured out. Michael Jackson writes the letters "EDIT" (publication) in capitals. It is about observing what is happening on earth. There is a lack of reverence and respect. Instead

death and destruction reign, screaming and begging. He calls for humility, bends his knees. Sathya Sai Baba gives us a guideline:

You are easily mislead by the machinations of the mind. Therefore I say "WATCH!" W stands for: "Watch your Words", A stands for "Watch your Actions", T stands for "Watch your Thoughts", C stands for "Watch your Character" and H stands for "Watch your Heart." When the watch reminds you every second of the necessity to observe these five, you can become quite happy.
Sathya Sai Baba Speaks, Vol. 6., p. 7*

7. The cycle ends with the phase of re-creation. The newsman can no longer bear to report what is happening. He feels empathy, feels the madness. It is necessary that the old things are destroyed so that new things can rise. Humility in front of the child, who is actually the only bearer of hope. Dignity is re-discovered. The "scream" crumbles. Finally everything is steadied and ends with an embrace. The scream dissolves and creation can be completed – the seventh day.

The game of life on the level of balance, where there are two in one - victor and vanquished, searcher and searched, joy and pain - is completed. I become the victor and the vanquished. I become the lover and the beloved. I become the master and the slave.
Michael Jackson, The Dance, Dancing the Dream

The symbolism of the number seven is very complex. Magician Merlin in the saga of King Arthur created magically a castle in the woodland of Broceliante within seven days, where miracles are hidden behind every bush and which never was left by anyone without the permission of Merlin" (Kübler, p. 44*). There are 49 knights, 7 times 7, who take their places at the table, which "will be once the center of the world" and where "will be seated the bravest knights of the world." "In the last chair indeed nobody is allowed to take their place. For a long time it will be called the 'Dangerous Seat,' because it is determined for someone who will yet be born" (Kübler, p. 54*).

This birth is the "realization of the Self"; it is called the second birth by Master Eckehart, the birth out of the world, and also the deeper meaning of Christmas. In the Revelation are mentioned the seven seals. In Genesis, seven days before the Flood God gives Noah the order to take seven of each of the pure animals into the ark, yet from the impure only two (Genesis 7:2). And in Genesis 41:25-27 we read: "Now Joseph said to Pharaoh, 'Pharaoh's dreams are one and the same; God has told Pharaoh what He is about to do. The seven good cows are seven years, and the seven good ears are seven years, the dreams are one and the same. The seven lean and ugly cows that came up after them are seven years, and the seven thin ears scorched by the east wind will be seven years of famine."

Seven is a prime number. We know four phases of the moon, each lasting seven days. Every seven years all cells of the body are renewed. The music of the spheres embraces seven octaves. The scale of colors has four segments. There is the seventh day of rest in Christianity and Islam. The seven-branched menorah in the Jewish tradition. The seven portals of Theben. The Seven Sisters, Pleiades, Seven Heavens. Teresa from Avila talks about seven homes. The Seven Wise Men. Seven world Seas. Seven World Wonders. Seven Great Rishis (Seers). Seven cosmic rays. Seven Manus. The seven-headed snake (Churchward, p. 175). The Tarot is based on the seven. In the "secret teachings" are described seven states of consciousness (Blavatsky). Anyone who is curious enough can find sufficient stuff for an exciting exploratory journey of the secrets of the Seven.

"All attempts to define the transpersonal consciousness as transformation in one step from the I encapsulated in the skin to the nice world soul have only wreaked havoc. It is precisely not a one-step process but at least a seven-step process. At least seven pivot points, seven profound changes of paradigm are necessary until one will reach the realization of the world soul (Wilber, 1997, p. 266*).
What is the origin of man? At the beginning there is the space, garbha in Sanskrit, which means germ or womb. In this womb life develops and has the form of a blister on the seventh day.
*Sathya Sai Baba, Sanathana Sarathi, 04/1997**

Seven is the sum of three and four. Three is the symbol for the divine and four the symbol for the human. The seven symbolizes the way of the transformation of the human to the divine and the symbol of completion. Michael Jackson shows us the way to this transformation and completion in "The Man in the Mirror":

If you wanna make the world a better place take a look at yourself and make a change.

If you want to make the world a better place, you have to work on yourself and change first. It's the same thing Kennedy was talking about when he said: "Ask not what your country can do for you; ask what you can do for your country." If you want to make the world a better place, take a look at yourself and make a change. Start with the man in the mirror. Start with yourself....Start with you. That's the truth. That's what Martin Luther King meant and Gandhi too. That's what I believe.

Michael Jackson, Moonwalk, p. 265, 268

Sathya Sai Baba's message is the same:

What man nowadays needs is the longing for unity in the diversity. Human beings are like the limbs in the social body. They are an integral part of society. Society is a part of nature and nature is a part of God. The integral an organic relation between man and God and between society and nature has to be understood precisely....To change society the first condition is individual change. Clean your heart, then society will be cleaned too.

Sathya Sai Baba, Sanathana Sarathi, 02/1998*

28. Dance of Life

The world we live in is the dance of the creator. Dancers come and go in the twinkling of an eye, but the dance lives on.
Michael Jackson, The Dance, Dancing the Dream

Come, let us dance the Dance of Creation. Let us celebrate the Joy of Life.
Michael Jackson, Heaven is Here, Dancing the Dream

Dolphins love to dance - of all creatures in the sea, that's their mark. Asking nothing from us, they cavort in the waves while we marvel. They race ahead of ships, not to get there first but to tell us, "It's all meant to be play. Keep to your course, but dance while you do it."
Michael Jackson, Enough for Today, Dancing the Dream

Love is a game. Play it!
Sathya Sai Baba, Sanathana Sarathi, 02/1998

The stars...are dancing too, doing a soft molecular jiggle that makes my carbon atoms jump in time. With my arms flung wide, I head for the sea, which brings out another dance in me. Moon dancing is slow inside, and soft as blue shadows on the lawn....a swirling nebula says, "Fast now, twirl!"...I start to spin as wildly as I can. This is my favorite dance, because it contains a secret. The faster I twirl, the more I am still inside. My dance is all motion without, all silence within....And

159

silence is my real dance....I know my fate is to show others that this silence, this light, this blessing is my dance.
Michael Jackson, Dance of Life, Dancing the Dream

In my veins I've felt the mystery....Life songs of ages throbbing in my blood have danced the rhythm of the tide and flood.
Michael Jackson, Planet Earth, Dancing the Dream

This sense of "the world in me" is how I always want to feel. That one in the mirror has his doubts sometimes. So I am tender with him. Every morning I touch the mirror and whisper, "Oh, friend, I hear a dance. Will you be my partner? Come."
Michael Jackson, That One in the Mirror, Dancing the Dream

The research of the subatomic world has shown that these descriptions of the dance are
not only allegoric, but that matter is really an energy dance. "These interactions represent an unceasing flow of energy....The interaction of the particles creates the stable structure which constructs the world, which in turn don't keep in line, but oscillate in rhythmic movements. Thus the whole universe is in constant movement and activity, in a permanent cosmic dance of energy." (Capra, p. 223*).

Physics speaks of the double nature of light as particle and wave. Man also is of double nature, as form and formless, material and spiritual, matter and energy. All these are different expressions of the unity, the Self.

This body of mine is a flux of energy in the river of time. Eons pass, ages come and go. I appear and disappear, playing hide-and-seek in the twinkling of an eye. I am the particle, I am the wave whirling at lightning speed....I am the Primeval Self in you and I.....In infinite expressions I come and go.

Experiments with a particle accelerator have shown that matter is created incessantly and decomposed incessantly. Modern physics has shown that rhythm and movement are basic marks of matter.
What scientists call matter is nothing but energy. An object appears as matter. But later it changes to energy. In a similar way someone may appear to you as an individual. But this also will turn to energy in due time. Therefore all forms and names you see are manifestations of energy.
What is this energy? It is something you cannot see nor hear nor comprehend with the mind. Energy is only energy. It is Divine. Every physical object has a base. In man there is electrical energy. In the same way there is radiant energy in man. There has to be a base for all this energy. God is the base for all the energy in the cosmos. The Veda has called this energy "transcendental energy." The names which are used may vary, but the substance is one and the same.
Sathya Sai Baba, Sanathana Sarathi, 08/1997*

And this substance dances - as already the name in German indicates (Subs-tanz - Tanz=dance) - cosmic dance. It is not substance in the limited sense of physics, matter or material, but in the original sense of metaphysics, the essence of all things, the primal ground of all being - that which lies under the dance).

The presence rises, shimmering with light. I could be in it forever, it is so loving and warm. But touch it once, and light shoots forth from the stillness. It quivers and thrills me, and I know my fate is to show others that this silence, this light, this blessing is my dance. I take the gift only to give it again.
Michael Jackson, Dance of Life, Dancing the Dream

All processes on the molecular and atomic levels as well as on the level of manifestation are components of the universe and partake in the cosmic dance. The visible stream of life we call man is made of energy, which manifests itself in different degrees of density. The visible physical body is the most dense one, and then follow in decreasing degrees the vital body, the emotional body and the mental body. The subtlety increases in the higher bodies, which are part of the divine world and which envelop and permeate the lower bodies. "According to the theory of fields every particle 'sings its eternal song' and produces rhythmic energy structures in "dense and subtle form" (Capra, p. 242*).

The concept of the cosmic dance is represented in Hinduism by the dancing Shiva. The ancient seers knew due to their inner vision that all life comes from Brahman, from pure absolute Being. In the holy Gospels and the fine arts the dancing Shiva, called Nataraja, is considered the Master of the World Stage. He embodies the third aspect of the trinity, the aspect of destruction and dissolution. "In the famous illustrations a foot of Shiva squashes the demon Mujalaka, the symbol for ignorance and worldliness....The dance happens in the matter, in the physicality individually as cosmically" (Lexikon der östlichen Weisheitslehren*). Shiva means literally "benevolent and rich in blessings." Which blessing is he granting? Which ignorance and worldliness is he squashing?

Michael Jackson talks about this multiplicity of the dancers who come and go, and about the experience that all is one. What remains when there is no longer a coming and going, no longer an up and down, no longer a back and forth, no longer a to and fro? Only the Self...

29. Balance, Serenity, Egality

Pure unbounded consciousness, truth, existence, Bliss am I.
Michael Jackson, Are you Listening? Dancing the Dream

When motionless consciousness is set in motion, there emerge life, forms and multiplicity, which manifest themselves in endless cycles of creation and destruction, birth and death. The manifold phenomena in the world of manifestation are illusions of the senses and mind, maya in Sanskrit, because they have no permanent base; they come and go. "This teaching takes the phenomena in this universe for a big illusion and a body is nearer to reality the closer it is to the UNKNOWN SUBSTANCE. For thus it is more distant to the world of maya, illusion" (Blavatsky, p. 94*).

Ignorant people fall prey to the spell of the maya and take the unreal for real and the real for unreal. Real or true is only that which is enduring, which always remains the same, which is timeless and unchanged. That is the motionless Brahman, the Absolute, the Void, the Formless, from which all forms emerge. Michael Jackson talks about this formlessness in "Are you Listening?":

In infinite expressions I come and go, playing hide-and-seek...I am...the void of space...I am the phenomenon, the field, the space...I am the Primeval Self in you and I.
Michael Jackson, Are you Listening? Dancing the Dream

Man experiences himself as separated and marked off from others, because his perception and awareness are directed to forms instead of to the Self. The five senses belong to the gross realm; the gross can never perceive the subtle, but only the other way around. Spiritual science knows five elements, which compose everything. The grossest is the earth, followed by water, fire and air. These four elements correspond with the four lower bodies, the physical, the vital, emotional and mental bodies. The subtle element, ether or space, called akasha in Sanskrit, corresponds to the higher bodies or worlds and pervades all lower bodies and worlds. It is all pervading and omnipresent. It knows no limits and no barriers and is subtler than air. The earth corresponds to the visual sense, the element water to the sense of taste, the element fire to the sense of smell, the element air to the sense of touch and the element space to the sense of hearing. The sense of hearing, which perceives sound, is the most subtle sense and is the connection to the divine world. "In the beginning was the word," say the Gospels (John 1:1), which means that the gross world has its origin in the subtle word. And this word or sound connects us with the origin. Music is harmonic and rhythmic sound. This is expressed in dictions like, "that's music to my ears." Disharmonic music is an abuse of the holy and healing quality of sound.

The way to our destination, being really human, is leading through these worlds. The pilgrim cannot plan when he will reach the destination. He heads on the path and at some time - when the wanderer is ready and prepared - it happens that he reaches his destination. Then the spiritual fire, the spiritual light sparks off, inflames and blazes up. That is what is called illumination, the realization of the SELF.

There is a Vedic ritual - agnihotra in Sanskrit - where two pieces of wood are so long rubbed each to the other until a flame arises. The fire is already latently existent in the wood, but can only be revealed when the rubbing is intense and persistent. In human life this rubbing corresponds to the encounter of the material and spiritual worlds.

Michael Jackson tells us the story of the fish which was thirsty. In his dream a baby fish was given the order from God to convey to the other fish in the ocean that he was thirsty. The little fish obeyed the order and harvested the most differing reactions from the others: rejection, spite, devaluation, until he met an old whale, which recognized: You have seen God, haven't you? And then he explained to the puzzled baby fish that we are searching for God at the wrong places. "'How strange,' the little fish said, 'to miss what is everywhere.' 'Very strange,' the old whale agreed. 'Doesn't it remind you of fish who say they're thirsty?'"

164

Michael Jackson, The fish that was thirsty, Dancing the Dream

In the beginning God is standing distant and observing your trials....When you cast off your attachment to the material world and direct yourself to doing good and service to the community, God will come encouragingly close. He is like the God of the Sun who is waiting outside of the closed door, like a servant who is staying at his place. He does not announce his presence and does not knock at the door. He is only waiting. When then the master will open the door only a gap, the sun will immediately flow in and dispel the darkness. When you ask God to help you he is at your side in an instant with arms wide open to help you. All you need is the ability to discriminate to pray to God and the wisdom to remember Him. Sathya Sai Baba, Sanathana Sarathi, 02/1998*

30. Truth

I was born...to speak the truth and never lie.
Michael Jackson, Ecstasy, Dancing the Dream

Every human being has his origin in truth. He is sustained by truth and he merges into truth. He is the embodiment of truth.
Sathya Sai Baba, Sanathana Sarathi, 01/1998*

I have to search for the truth in all things.
Michael Jackson , People 10/1987

I don't sing it if I don't mean it.
Michael Jackson, Moonwalk

In this way Michael Jackson talked even as a young boy; in HIStory we can hear his childlike voice with the following confession:
What one wishes is to be touched by truth and to be able to interpret that truth so that one may use what one is feeling and experiencing, be it despair or joy, in a way that will add meaning to one's life and will hopefully touch others as well. This is art in its highest form. These moments of enlightenment are what I continue to live for.
Michael Jackson, Moonwalk, p. 285

Let's dream of a tomorrow...where we know the highest truth in the heart of all creation.
Michael Jackson, Cover of Dangerous album

Mankind lost heaven when the ego started to reign and prove that God does not exist. Thus also paradise was lost. The ego, which believes in the existence of many other egos, has chosen competition, rivalry, war and the fight for dominance as its purpose. Separation and limitation produce suffering, pain and pressure. The original Fall of man is the collective amnesia of the self, the obliviation of his identity. To solve the whole tragedy there is nothing to do but to realize and acknowledge again the state of innocence, to re-member the self and to start back to our legacy as "Son of God." The Christian term "Son of God" means Divine Incarnation. The Hindus call it an Avatar. Every human being is a Divine Incarnation and is called to know it and realize it. We only need to awaken and realize that there is nothing to do besides staying awake and to re-member our true Self permanently - at each time and at each place: "I AM the way and the truth and life" (John 14:6), as Jesus assured us.

"A woman lay in coma. Suddenly she felt as if she were entering heaven and standing in front of the judgment seat. "Who are you?", a voice asked. "I am the wife of the Mayor," she answered. "I did not ask whose wife you are, I asked you who you are." "I am mother of four children." "I did not ask your whose mother you are, but who you are." "I am a teacher." "I did not ask for your profession, but who you are." In this way it continued. Everything she replied did not seem a satisfying answer to the question, "Who are you?". "I am Christian." "I did not ask for your religion, but who you are." I am the one who went to church every day and helped the poor and needy." "I don't ask what you did, but who you are?" Obviously she did not pass the test, because she was sent back to earth. After she recovered she decided to find out who she is. And that was the whole difference. (Anthony de Mello, cit. in "Who am I?"*)

31. Bliss

The knowledge or realization of the self is the "ignition of the light of the soul" (Schmidt*) and is accompanied by equanimity, serenity and bliss. Joy and suffering are overcome and give way to a state of consciousness which cannot be described in words. It is bliss which is not incited by outer events or actions and then perishes, but it is steadily flowing inside. To find it, it is necessary to master the lower bodies, dissolve destructive emotions and to tame the restless mind. In its stead there follow empathy, unconditional love, compassion, humility and inner and outer peace, and soon after acceptance of all that is, without critique, without judgment, without evaluation, without etiquette, without classification. It is as it is! Michael Jackson knows this state at least since the birth of his son Prince, when he was "24 hours of the day in a state of bliss" (Life, Nov 1994,.p. 92f)

From Bliss I came

In Bliss I am sustained

To Bliss I return

Michael Jackson, Are you Listening? Dancing the Dream

For we were born...to live in bliss

Michael Jackson, Ecstasy, Dancing the Dream

In your beauty I have known the how

Of timeless bliss, this moment of now.

Michael Jackson, Planet Earth, Dancing the Dream

We are like ripples

In the vast Ocean of Consciousness...

Heaven is Here

Right now is the moment
of Eternity
Don't fool yourself
Reclaim your Bliss

Michael Jackson, Heaven is Here, Dancing the Dream

"Heaven is Here, there is no other place" (Course in Miracles, Handbook for teachers, 6, 4-5).
Children of the world, we'll do it - with song and dance and innocent bliss...
We'll do it - Children of the world, we'll do it - with song and dance and innocent bliss...

Michael Jackson, Children of the World, Dancing the Dream

Those are moments when babies smile...
Those are moments we're one with God...
We can only win, we have felt the glimmer
In the bliss
We're floating awhile

Michael Jackson, When babies smile, Dancing the Dream

Michael also cites the example of the holy Teresa, who confessed her experience: "As if I were carried off by an eagle my ecstasy lifted me into the air."

In everything of creation bliss is imminent, as bliss is the universal Absolute. Everything is being-awareness-bliss, and that means: divine, sat-cit-ananda in Sanskrit. Everything IS, Isness is being which is capable of coming into being....The ability to be realized and to realize, to be aware and to grant awareness is called cit in Sanskrit....The third proof for our innate divinity is our

inner yearning for bliss. Without exception everyone is motivated by this yearning for bliss.
Sathya Sai Baba Speaks, Vol. 16, chap. 30*

Love is my form
Truth is my breath
bliss is my sustenance

My life is my message
Expansion is my life

Love needs no reason
love needs no time
no birth, no death.
Sathya Sai Baba, Sanathana Sarathi, 12/1998

32. The plan of the prophet

In the moment of birth the memory of our origin gets lost. All the more important it is to give the newborn homunculus safety, protection and love, as without the knowledge about his divine home he feels alone and abandoned. He has come to re-gain the knowledge of the truth about him within a physical body and to no more forget it. We cannot foresee how often the individual soul has to start the journey on earth to complete this mission. The cycle of birth and death will end when His will is done and His will and his will are one; that means when the ego is crucified. The ego with the name "i," which has made itself an idol, has to be crossed out cleanly, so that the "I," also named Christ, can resurrect. Jesus is the human aspect of this allegory, and Christ is the divine aspect of every lifestream, who has come more than 2000 years ago to re-mind humanity about its origin and true identity. Jesus and Christ are one and have to be realized as One in everyone. When man finds his childhood and innocence again the re-membrance will return. There is no other way, for only the childlike innocent part of us has the knowledge, the creativity and the power to complete the search for the Self. When the ego recedes, the I instead of the i can take the lead. This I has a stamina which will resist all aggressors and adversaries. Michael Jackson is aware of this fact.

I love children, as you can see, and babies. Well, there's a certain sense that animals and children have that...gives me a certain force that later on in adulthood is lost because of the conditioning that happens in the world. A great poet said once, "When I see children I see that God has not yet given up on man." An Indian poet from India said that, and his name is Tagore. The innocence of children represents to me the source of infinite creativity. That is the potential of every human being. But by the time you are an adult, you're conditioned, you're so conditioned by the things about you and it goes.

Michael Jackson, Ebony May 1992

The holy scriptures of India teach that God has a thousand eyes, a thousand hands and a thousand feet. That means that we meet God in every human. God himself cannot act in this world, because He is formless. But He expresses himself in all and every form. When man subordinates his self-will, which creates only sorrow and suffering, His will will be done and then the divine plan for planet earth and humanity can be fulfilled. Michael Jackson follows this vision despite all resistance and obstacles.

I am a visionary and I am very resilient. I feel as if I have a suit of armor around me, like a rhinoceros skin. I am here to do what I am supposed to do.

Michael Jackson, Internet Simulchat, 17th of Aug. 1995*

Also Robert F. Kennedy was driven by Spirit. Michael cites his motto: "There are people who see things as they are and ask 'Why?'. I dream of things that are not and ask 'Why not?'".

To express this great soul everybody has to start with himself and transform his consciousness. The recipe for this is: Everything which you meet is your mirror. When we want to be whole and complete, we have to stop projecting our self onto others and admit that everything that we meet outside is a mirror of our inside. The wisdom of the mirror can help us to see more clearly.

33. Wisdom of the mirror

Everything which man perceives outside him is a projection of his inner world. Man is only able to see the things which are inherent in himself, as the outer is merely a mirror which shows man himself. Knowing and observing the laws of the mirror allows man to spend his time on planet earth for his own end and approach himself to his Self. Everything else is a waste of time.

First law of the mirror
Everything that disturbs or irritates me in another person and what I want to change in him is something which I have within me.

Second law of the mirror
When I am hurt by what others criticize or fight at myself and I feel insulted, then I am affected and not "neutral." Then I have not yet solved and released the concerned things in me, but deny or block me of the feelings. My ego is strong.

Third law of mirror
When I am not emotionally touched by what others criticize or fight at myself and their words do not stir me up, then the concerned things are his own picture and inner world, which he is only projecting on me.

Fourth law of mirror
Everything I love in others I am myself. I recognize myself in the other one - we are one in these aspects.

Michael Jackson speaks it out:
I'm starting with the man in the mirror. I'm asking him to change his ways. And no message could have been any clearer. If you wanna make the world a better place take a look at yourself and make a

173

change. I'm gonna make a change, it's gonna feel real good.... That's why I'm starting with me....I'm asking him to change his ways.

Michael Jackson, Man in the Mirror

34. Life is One

...when I'm dancing, I've felt touched by something sacred. In those moments, I've felt my spirit soar and become one with everything that exists.
Michael Jackson, Dancing the Dream, Dancing the Dream

There is only one Wholeness, only one Mind....And you and I were never separate. It's just an illusion.
Michael Jackson, Heaven is Here, Dancing the Dream

You create the world of your choice. You see many because you are looking for many, not for the one. Try to subsume the many under the one, your physical body and that of others, the family, the village, the community, the state, the nation, the world. This way...you will reach the state of oneness in thought, word and deed. That is the practice of love, because love is expansion, inclusion and mutuality. Man has to become a universal and expansive being, until he embodies the whole creation.
Sathya Sai Baba, Sanathana Sarathi, 08/1997*

I believe that...the purpose of every art is the union of spiritual and material, of the divine and the human.
Michael Jackson, Oprah Winfrey Show, 10th of Feb. 1993

I keep on dancing and then, it is the eternal dance of creation. The creator and creation merge into one wholeness of joy. I keep on dancing and dancing......and dancing, until there is only......the dance.
Michael Jackson, Dancing the Dream, Dancing the Dream

This is the same as the view of a master of Zen: "When I heard the sound of the ringing bell, there was no longer an I and no longer a bell, only belling." (Wilber 1997, p. 295*).

The whirling dervishes, an order in the Sufi tradition, which was founded by the mystic Jelalu'ddin Rumi in the 13th century, practice their dancing rituals even today. They whirl for hours counterclockwise around their body axis. The dance facilitates the breakthrough to higher cosmic dimensions. The whirling direction to the left causes the accumulated energy to move centripetally and they can break through the limits of earthly time and enter eternal time - **presence**.

Observing Michael Jackson dancing on stage and in his short films, we will notice that he is always is whirling counterclockwise around his body axis.

But for me the sweetest contact with God has no form. I close my eyes, look within, and enter a deep soft silence. The infinity of God's creation embraces me. We are one.

Michael Jackson, God, Dancing the Dream

With these words Michael tries to express his experiences beyond words. People who have headed on the journey inwards will recognize the landscape, the place where opposites are annihilated, where silence and sound, immobility and dance, passivity and activity, subject and object are one.

I am the thinker, the thinking, the thought. I am the seeker, the seeking, the sought.

Michael Jackson, Are you Listening? Dancing the Dream

There is no need for man to search for something outside himself. The whole universe is within him, in his heart.

*Sathya Sai Baba, Sanathana Sarathi, 02/1998**

This knowledge reveals itself when we look with the eye of wisdom, which looks through material bodies and perceives the Divine in all and everything. The term "alone" creates fear, because we feel separated when identified with the physical body. On the level of the soul, when we see with the heart, we feel that we are not alone, but all one.

Your angel is a speck of light perched at the very center of your heart. It is smaller than an atom, but just wait. Once you get close to it, your angel will expand. The closer you come, the more it will grow, until finally, in a burst of light, you will see your angel in its true shape, and at that very instant, you will also see yourself.

Michael Jackson, Angel of Light, Dancing the Dream

Those are moments when babies smile. Those are moments when we're one with God....In silent reflection we feel our perfection. We are the source, we are the crucible. Nothing can hurt us, for we are invincible. There is no sin, there is no sinner.

Michael Jackson, When Babies Smile, Dancing the Dream

The Veda describes the Divine as "smaller than the smallest atom and bigger than the biggest object." Many look at the atom as something which is invisible to the eye. That is not correct. The atom consists of particles which are invisible. The ancients believed that the divine is eminent in the atom....For centuries the scientists have been trying to explore the nature of the atom. But a very long time ago, already Prahlada, a young lad, knew that God is emanent in the atom and proclaimed this message.

Sathya Sai Baba, Sanathana Sarathin, 04/1997*

The kingdom inside has various names: Great Silence, Heaven, Holy Heart, secret Place of the Highest, True Home, Power of Love, Almighty Presence and many more. All these names indicate the same place, where every human being is heading, be it consciously or unconsciously.

Michael Jackson challenges us in his art to put the questions and seek the answers which bring us nearer to this truth. For example the film "Teaser" is studded with symbols, whereby one has to observe the film again and again to decipher them and one will discover new aspects every time.

We see people working by the sweat of their brows in a foundry. A pentagram in a circle. Marching soldiers in uniforms from North Korea with Russian writing on their arms: **"Why do we live when we will die?"** Boots marching in step. A standard with the text: **"Why do we live when we will die?"** Chains. An eye without a pupil. Instruments. A roll. Star and cross. Michael's upper body with the pentagram on his arm. Outstretched arms. Boots marching in step. Faces. Michael's right fist with bandaged arm. A woman fainting, missing power (wordplay in German: Ohnmacht - ohne Macht = without power). Michael takes off his mirrored glasses. Shouting fans. A sign "King of Pop." Michael's face, it is raining confetti. Michael throws kisses to the crowd with his right hand, which is covered by a black glove, with shining face. Shouting fans show a V, the victory sign. Helicopters are circling in front of the sun disc, three helicopters in front of the silhouette of a tower. Running people with flags. A lantern emitting sparks. Fire. Headlights. Running people are stopped. Headlights enlighten a huge veiled statue. Helicopters are circling. Faces full of expectation are looking upwards, holding candles in their hands. A man is rappeling the statue. Helicopters circling. Children with candles. A man with targeting glasses. Dynamite explodes. The ties of the statue break. Boulders are falling. Children with candles are waving. Helicopters circling. The veil falls down. The statue is in full the light. Michael Jackson appears like "a phoenix from the ashes" (Brown, p. 130). Children are shouting and waving. A woman without power is carried away. Helicopters circling around the statue. Sign "God". The arm of the statue shows the pentagram. Fire sparkles. A boy shouts, "Michael I love you." Helicopters starting between the legs of the statue. Shouting children. Helicopters spraying powder and confetti. The arms of the children are reaching out. Radiant faces. Children embrace each other. In between policemen. A litter. Radiant faces. The face of the statue and spraying helicopters.

178

Why do we live when we will die?

The answer to this ancient question of man we will not find in books and not in the reports of other people. Their knowledge can only encourage us to head on the journey ourselves. When we then have arrived at our Self then we know what Master Eckehart wants to say: "Man is born twice, once into the world and once out of the world." After the birth we stand up like a "Phoenix from the ashes" and know that we will never die.

Beyond all hearing, beyond all seeing, in the core of your Being, is a field that spans infinity. Unbounded pure is the embryo of divinity. If we could for one moment BE, in an instant we would see a world where no one has suffered or toiled, of pristine beauty never soiled, of sparkling waters, singing skies, of hills and valleys where no one dies.

That enchanted garden, that wondrous place where we once frolicked in times of grace. In ourselves a little deep, in that junkyard in that heap, beneath that mound of guilt and sorrow, is the splendor of another tomorrow. If you still have promises to keep, just take that plunge, take that leap.

Michael Jackson, Quantum leap, Dancing the Dream

35. Magic

Magical child once felt a twinge, a faint recollection, a memory unhinged. In the colors, the forms, the hue there seemed a mystery with a subtle clue. Behind the wind, the storm, the gale, within the shroud, beyond the veil, hidden from view in a wondrous pattern, there seemed a force that he could not fathom....He danced in bliss...Strangers came...Despite their attacks, they could not break...God's gift of love...not knowing his strength or what he sought to seek...but the mysterious force just kept its hold....Magical child...diving deep into his soul...in his Self was infinite scope....In that silence beyond all seeing was a field...of power, of awesome glory.

Michael Jackson, Magical Child, part 2, Dancing the Dream

What is the meaning of magic? "There is widely disagreement about the definition of the term 'magic'...Many people still have the childish idea that it is about some sort of circus wizardry. The linguistic root of this often misused word "maj" means "great," "royal" and similar highest forms of being. Magic in the original sense is "mastery" or holding control of the states of the own "i" before one thinks about controlling something else." (Tart, p. 543*)

My idea of magic doesn't have much to do with stage tricks and illusions. The whole world abounds in magic....Nature (is) the best of all magicians.

Michael Jackson, Magic, Dancing the Dream

Magical child was ready to bow, sow the seed, pick up the plough, with effortless ease, without a sigh, without a tear, without a cry....to sing together as one race.

Michael Jackson, Magical Child, part 2, Dancing the Dream

Magic overcomes separation. In a vision Isaiah (2:4) realized: "They will beat their swords into plowshares and their spears into pruning hooks. Nation will not take up sword against nation, nor will they train for war anymore."

Create a world with no fear. Together we'll cry happy tears, see the nations turns their swords into plowshares.

Michael Jackson, Heal the World, HIStory album

A child's mind needs the nourishment of mystery, magic, wonder, and excitement.

Michael Jackson, On Children of the World, Dancing the Dream

As soon as we find the magic child inside ourselves the problems that pressure the world will solve themselves. The factors of power and greed will no longer shape the action and thinking of man, but sharing and giving will prevail. An ethic and moral, which is imposed from outside, is superfluous, as the sense for dignity, equality and inner greatness operates naturally in every human being, without the necessity of being taught and learned. The wish to serve and share will determine the life of all and everyone. These conditions no longer allow war or fight, because there is no sense of separation, no hate, no greed and no struggle for power anymore. When love takes over and mounts the throne, then the old illusionary ego construction will collapse like a bubble, because it is not fed with energy anymore. One who is able to take the sword EXCALIBUR out of the anvil is the righteous heir of the crown and the throne. The sword is the symbol for the spiritual and the anvil the symbol for the material. The spiritual is anchored in the material and can only be extracted when our thinking, feeling and doing is purified, free from the six enemies: fear, envy, hate, greed, delusion and pride. When the inner enemies are conquered we have the right to miracles.

Michael Jackson shouts out his message to the world: "To care, especially for the children," "to make the world a better place," "to bring harmony to the world," "to fulfill the plan of the prophet," "to find again the place of love." And in the video "Earth Song" he shows us that the creator answers our pleading, when it comes from the bottom of our soul and we trust that it will be answered. We see how people from all corners of the world are humbly hitting the dirt, digging their fingers into the soil pleading for redemption. The creator answers their pleading and reverses the process of destruction, so that the trees are standing up and life is returning into dead bodies. Faith can move mountains.

I don't accept you telling me that you are atheists without believing in the Lord. Because what is the root of believing in yourself? Who are you to not believe in yourself? No, you believe in yourself because your Self is God and you have an unshakeable believing in God, deep within. Believing in God and believing in your Self are identical.
Sathya Sai Baba Speaks, Vol. 2*

36. Silence - OM

One who knows does not speak, one who speaks does not know.
Chuang tzu

The talking of such fault-finders is like the sound of bronze. Metals without value make noise; gold, which does not make noise, has a great value. True knowing is mute, it follows the path of silence. Don't allow that the words of these bronze-sounding people enter into your ears, but fill them with the cosmic primal sound of OM.
Sathya Sai Baba, Answers, p. 100*

The only way to persuade the ignorant sometimes is silence. When people come together most keep talking unceasingly. Many feel uncomfortable when there is no talking. They call it "awkward silence." At the beginning of therapeutic groups we can regularly observe the phenomenon that participants are uneasily fidgeting on their chairs, when there has been nobody talking for some minutes. There are participants who cannot bear the situation and want to leave the room. What is the reason that they are unable to stay in silence? Why are we incessantly talking? When there is much talk it does not mean that there is much said. By silence there can be said much more.

I thought about all this, about how generations once lived in harmony with the earth, leaving no marks to scar the places they inhabited. At camp that night I said, "You left out one thing." "What's that?" he asked. "Where are the Ancient Ones buried?"

Without reply, he poked his stick into the fire. A bright flame shot up, licked the air, and disappeared. My teacher gave me a glance to ask if I understood this lesson. I sat very still, and my silence told him I did.

Michael Jackson, Mark of the Ancients, Dancing the Dream

Newton, who for his entire life was ambitious, and who for a long time did not want to share his discoveries with anybody, turned humble until shortly before his death, and he wrote: "I don't know how the world will see me, I see myself only as a little boy playing at the beach and enjoy up and then to discover an extraordinary beautiful pebble or an especially nice shell, while the great **ocean of truth** is lying before him totally unexplored" (Sagan, p. 82*).

This ocean of energy, this unity, this void, this nothingness has been postulated by teachers of wisdom for eons. It was given many names like brahman (the absolute) and atman (the individual) in the Vedas, the Tao in Taoists, the Dharmakaya of the Buddhists, Ahura Mazda by the Parsi, Jehovah by the Jews, the God of the Christians and Allah in Islam, the Logos of the Initiated and Ain-Soph of the Cabbalists.

Confusion is only a result when the levels are confused. A statement on the level of the explicit is not necessarily valid on the level of the implicit or the void. For that reason Charles Tart demanded a sciences oriented at the state of consciousness.

The wise have declared: That which is finer than the finest and vaster than the vastest and which is ever present everywhere as the eternal witness, that is the atman. The atman is the atom and the atom is the atman. All three terms - brahman, atman and atom - refer to one and the same thing.
Sathya Sai Baba, Sanathana Sarathi, 08/1997*

At this point the line to modern times is drawn. The ancient mystical terms of Sanskrit, brahman and atman, are identical with the scientific term atom. The atomic and subatomic sciences are coming - without knowing it themselves - very near to the truth. The only reason that science cannot easily discover truth is the fact that science is not really free, but using concepts and constructs. "To realize the Self, you have to forget everything" (Asthavakragita, p. 30*).

There is an ancient ritual of initiation to true knowing:
Question: In what do you trust?
Answer: I only trust in the truth.

184

Question: What is truth?
Answer: (Silence)

Even this book is not able to answer the question: "What is truth?" But when it compels at least one reader to head on the path of searching for the truth, it has reached its goal.
In the western mystical tradition we know four principles to which the searcher for truth should adhere when he wants to avoid stumbling on this tightrope walk or going astray, which are:

Knowledge - Venture - Willing – Silence.

Entelechy - determined action which is inherent in everything - will take care that the plan of the prophet will be fulfilled, that the Great Work will be done. Man can contribute to accelerating it or slowing it down, but he will never not stop it. The time has come for him to support the universe instead of intervening as a hindering factor in the cosmic work. How long will it still take until man will decide to wake up instead of passing his time by trying to transform a nightmare in a comfortable dream - it remains still a dream.

Every child should sing together in harmony...all nations sing, let's harmonize all around the world.
Michael Jackson, HIStory

"The emanation of the power of divine love (is) the highest vibration which a lifestream can...achieve. It flows automatically through the lifestream, when it is qualified...with harmony, which is the channel for its flowing. It will automatically be cut from the lifestream every time, when it breaks the law of harmony and love." (Book of Life, p. 173*)

Mother dear, you gave me life...
And if I ever change this world
It's from the emotions you've unfurl'd

Your compassion is so sweet and dear
Your finest feelings I can hear
I can sense your faintest notion
The wondrous magic of your love potion.
Michael Jackson, Mother, Dancing the Dream

"We were told that an individual has to turn into the embodiment of love to heal. That is a scientific truth." (Book of Life, p. 174*) Everyone who has mastered his emotions and thoughts and is able to maintain inner harmony and equanimity - independent of what is happening in the outside world - can serve as a channel for the power of cosmic, unconditional, selfless love, which is the only power in the universe able to make a permanent difference and bring about transformation. When Michael Jackson fans turn into friends and follow his ideal - instead of his idol - when they turn into active collaborators at the giant task of transforming planet earth, then they have realized the message and themselves.

Some fans of Michael have to understand that their example and idol is not served when they idolize and divinize his personality, but are not aware of his message, his ideal and his inner essence. Such a view is nothing but idolatry, like the dance of the Israelites around the golden calf. The one who is occupied with outer things is not open to the power of love. Also the one who only soaks it up like a sponge to the point of bulging is only waiting until the sponge dries out. To again try to fill it is not serving the whole but behaving like a parasite. Parasites nurture themselves from the energy of other living beings. They suck them and misuse them without giving something in return. That attitude contradicts the universal law of life and leads to death and destruction.

37. Ten things you can do

1. Be thankful!
Thank for what the world is giving you each day. The air you breathe, the food you consume, the water you drink. Try to be aware once a day of the simple fact that the world is sustaining you.

2. Educate yourself!
Educate yourself unceasingly, while going through life. Learn as much as possible about yourself and others. Life is a journey which is enriched by ideas and the ability to share them with others.

3. Meditate!
The worlds begins inside yourself. Take some minutes every day to calm yourself. Listen to you inner voice. Know that you are connected with the universe as a whole.

4. Practice nonviolence!
Violence is the result of the sense of being of separated one from the other. Know that you are connected every day in manifold manner with the totality of the planet. Work to find solutions which benefit the whole.

5. Respect nature!
The planet is an intelligent organism. He thinks, he feels, he knows. Respect nature and nature will respect you.

6. Recycle!
We did not inherit this world. It is a loan from the future.

7. Touch upon things!
When you see an injustice speak about it. Often being silent is the bigger evil.

8. Travel!

To see the world opens your mind to the variety of cultures and customs. By traveling you become aware that we are sharing this world with all nations.

9. Serve!

Serving the next one begins at home, in your family and your community. Engage locally. The world is not a distant place, it begins where you are living.

10. Go to the polls!

If you are old enough to go to the polls, go! If you are not yet old enough, then learn how to participate in the polls. The right to choose is one of the biggest abilities of man. Use it to create a better future!

(Michael Jackson, Cited in "Sony Museum of HIStory", no longer available in the Internet*)

38. Ten directives

1. Look at the country in which you are born as holy. Behave in a patriotic manner towards your nation, but refrain from criticizing and humiliating other countries. Not even in your dreams you should think about causing harm to your country.

2. Respect all religions equally.

3. Realize the brotherhood of man. Treat all as brothers. Love all.

4. Maintain cleanliness in your house and environment, because that will foster hygiene and health and help you.

5. Practice charity, but don't support beggars by giving them money. Care for food, clothing and shelter and support them in other ways. (Don't support laziness).

6. Don't bribe others and don't let you be bribed. (Don't be misled to corrupt actions).

7. Tame envy and jealousy. Enhance your view and perception. Treat everyone alike, independent of origin and beliefs.

8. Try to do as much as possible yourself. When you are wealthy and have servants they can help you. But service for the community has to be done personally - by yourself.

9. Nourish and cherish love for God and fear of sin; avoid the sin.

10. Never violate the laws of the country; abide them faithfully. Be exemplary citizens.

Sathya Sai Baba

39. I

When God out from the burning bush was asked by Moses what he should reply to the Israelites when they asked for the name of who sent him, God identified himself as "Eheye ahse eheye", which means: "I AM THAT I AM" (Exodus 3:14).

"I AM" is name- and formless. The one whose consciousness has no idea and no access to the void does not know that every time he says "I am" adding a quality, he is speaking untruth and is limiting himself in ignorance. His limited ego is using the name I AM because it usurps God's place and tries to prove that God is not. There are other names for the nameless presence I AM which are not tied to the belief in a religion or in God: Higher Self, Higher Mind, Inner Master, Inner Voice, Consciousness (Drucker, 1997, Spezzano, 1996).

There never was a time when I was not or you were not. There never will be a time when we will cease to be.

Michael Jackson, Heaven is Here, Dancing the Dream

"You don't have a birthday, because you have always lived. Your were never born and you will never die. You are not the child of who you call mother and father, but their co-adventurer on a long journey to understand things as they are." (Bach, 1992*)

Only ignorance uses the "I" to indicate the body.
Sathya Sai Baba, Upanishad Vahini, p. 79

Jesus talked about this "I AM" to indicate to the divine spark in every human being. Jesus' message, "I am the way, the truth and life," talks about the divine principle inside everyone and is not related to the human being called Jesus. In relation to this principle Jesus said at the end of his passion: "I and the father are one."

190

"Pay attention to all the levels where the "I AM" is always present. Then you will soon realize that peace and bliss are your real nature. This nature will be disturbed by trying to reach it by any means. Stop disturbing it, that's all. There is no necessity to search for it. You would never search for something which is already yours. You yourself are God, the highest reality." (Nisargadatta, p. 132*)

When we look with the outer eyes we only see bodies, billions of bodies on this earth, according to the laws of the mind, $1+1+1+1+1=5$ etc. Each of these bodies labels itself as "i" and sees separate bodies. Thus everybody is speaking the same untruth by using the name "i" when referring to different bodies. I was blessed by grace to experience that i am not this small petty "i", but the vast great "I." For this I the formula $1+1=1+1=1+1=1+1=1$ is true or $1+1+1+1+1+1+ .... +1=1$.

"I am you, answered the light, and now come on." Thus ends the story of Michael Ende "Legend of the guideline".…."There are moments which stand vertical and unshakeable on the stream of time, which flows below it." (Ende, p. 282*)

Lao Tzu teaches in the "Tao Te Ching": "The tao begot one, one begot two, two begot three. And three begot the ten thousand things" (42).

When academic science focuses on and explores the visible, it is dealing with the two (the opposites, for example of dark and bright, of male and female, of positive and negative) and will never find the one.

"Then I abstract…with open eyes the subjective moment - the I AM or Atman element - from the wholeness of the manifold objective consciousness. That is my focus. Naturally I came across what is relative darkness and void. But I realized it to be absolute light and abundance and I realized that I was THAT. This aroused something in Merril-Wolf, which he called "quality of ambrosia," a state of pure joy and freedom." (Wolinsky, 1994, p. 11*)

The Vedas use the expression "amrita" to identify this "nectar of immortality," which is also known as "water of life" (Mittwede, p. 25).

Where time is not, immortality's clear.
Michael Jackson, Once we were There, Dancing the Dream

Unity and Oneness exist in the timeless realm. When someone forgets about something it does not change anything of the thing itself. A truth remains the truth, even if it is not realized as such. As long as man stays distant from the source, he is not able to realize the truth. To realize it he has to approximate the source. He who recedes from the fire will not feel the heat. And when he believes that heat does not warm up, it is due to his distance from it, but not due to the missing quality of the fire to heat up.

Due to the differences of outer physical forms you are victims of ignorance of your true self....One who describes oneself uses the term "I." "The principle of I is the principle of the Self. This Self is called Atman in Sanskrit.
Sathya Sai Baba, Sanathana Sarathi, 12/1997*

We will find the "I" when we look inwards instead of outwards, when we see with the heart, inwards, with in-sight.

The divine nature of the "I" has to be understood properly. The "I" is the master of the body, the senses and the mind.
Sathya Sai Baba, Sanathana Sarathin 12/1997*

The qualities of this "I" are love, wisdom, power. In Sanskrit it is called "hridaya", which means "heart" or literally "that which contains amiability." "Already in the Veda the heart is considered as the seat of the immortal soul of man" (Mittwede, p. 92*).

40. To my immortal soul

Awake!
Awake from the dull sleep of inertia,
Awake from the dull sleep of darkness,
Awake from the dull sleep of delusion!

Stand up, child of light,
Stand up, immortal soul,
Stand up, divine germ in all things!

Cut the ties of desires,
Cut the bonds of fear,
Cut the veils of ignorance!

Wake the radiant flame of devotion,
Wake the radiant flame of infinite empathy,
Wake the radiant flame of worldwide peace!

Realize my soul, that there is only the One,
Realize my soul, that you are part of the One,
Realize my soul, that you are the One!

You are free from thoughts,
You are free from desires,
You are free from illusions and delusions!

You are eternal infinite peace,
You are an infinite ocean of light,
You are one with all beings
You are sat-cit-ananda, being-consciousness-bliss!
Sathya Sai Baba

Thanks

I thank all the lovely souls
who are myself and serve as a mirror
for the Self,

who teach me
that you and I are one.
One and One is One ...

only One ...

How simple ... .

Namaste ... I love you

Margott Schuerings, August 2016

Bibliography

Ashtavakragita, Drucker, Al (Hrsg), Dietzenbach 1997

Bach, R., There's No Such Place As Far Away, London, 1992

Balsekar, R.S., Duett der Einheit, Bielefeld, 1991

Berendt, J.-E-, Ich höre - also bin ich, Goldmann, 1991

Bhagavadgita, Gesang des Erhabenen, Freiburg, 6. Aufl., 1994

Blavatsky, H.P., Die Geheimlehre, Wien, 1975

Brown, G., Michael Jackson & the J. Family, Omnibus Press, 1996

Capra, F., Das Tao der Physik, Scherz, 10. Aufl., 1988

Cayce, E., The Sleeping Prophet, 1991

Churchward, J., MU - der versunkene Kontinent, Aitrang, 1990

The Gospels

Drucker, Al, Ich bin, 4. erw. Aufl., 1997

DTV-Lexikon, Band 8, 14, 17, 1969

Easwaran, E., Der Mensch Gandhi, Herder, 1997

Ebmeier, J., Das Phänomen Michael Jackson, Hamburg, 1997

Ebony, May 1992

Ebony, Oct. 1994

Eckehart, Meister, Deutsche Predigten und Traktate, München, 1963

Ende, M., Die Legende vom Wegweiser

Esotera, 08/1999

Fanibundna, E., Vision of the Divine, Prashanti Nilayam,, 1976

Fox, S., Endlich aufgewacht, München, 3. Aufl., 1998

Gaulden, A., Geist-Wende, München, 1997

Ghooi, Ch., Spirituality and Health, Prasanthi Nilayam

Goethe, J.W., Faust

Grant, A., Michael Jackson - Die Chronik, Königswinter, 1997

Grof, St., Das Abenteuer der Selbstentdeckung, München, 1988

Haraldsson, E., Sai Baba - ein modernes Wunder, Freiburg, 1993

Hawkings, St., Kurze Geschichte der Zeit, Hamburg, 1992

Heindel, M., Die Weltanschauung der Rosenkreuzer oder mystisches Christentum, 1991

Hellinger, B., Ordnungen der Liebe, Heidelberg, 1995

Hesse, H., Siddharta, Frankfurt, 12. Aufl., 1997

Hislop, J., Gespräche mit Sathya Sai Baba, Dietzenbach, 5. Aufl., 1994

Huxley, A., Gott ist, DTV, 1996

I Ging, Diederichs, 4. Aufl., 1978

ICH, Apokalypse ist Zuversicht, 1997

Jackson, M., Moonwalk, cited here from Arrow books, 2010 (originally German edition, 1992)

Jackson, M., Dancing the Dream, American Edition, 1992

Jackson, M., Thriller, CD-Album, 1982

Jackson, M., Bad, CD-Album, 1987

Jackson, M., Dangerous, CD-Album, 1991

Jackson, M., HIStory, CD-Album, 1995

Jackson, M., Blood on the Dance Floor, CD-Album, 1997

Jackson, M., On the Line, Maxi CD, 1997

Jackson, M., The Complete, Intern. Music Publications, 1997

Jackson, M., 35. Grammy Awards, 24th Feb. 1992

Jackson, M., Performance in Pasadena, California, 31st Jan. 1993

Jackson, M., Talks to Oprah Winfrey, 10th Feb.1993

Jackson, M., Prime Time Live, 14th June 1995

Jackson, M., Simulchat, 17th Aug. 1995

Jackson, M., VH1, 10th Nov. 1996

Jackson, M., Interview with Ian Molly Meldrum, 19th Nov. 1996

Jackson, M., Interview OK Magazine, 4th April, 1997

Jackson, M., Interview OK Magazine, 11th April 1997

Jackson, M., ABC's 20/20, 12th Sept. 1997

Jackson, M., München, Hotel Bayerischer Hof, 25th March 1998

Jackson, M., HIStory Museum, Sony MJ Website (no longer available)

Jagadeesan, J., Speech 29th Nov. 1998, Prashanti Nilayam, India

Karanjia, R.K., Go lives in India, Prashanti Nilayam, 1994

Krystal, Ph., Monkey Mind, Seeshaupt-München, 1995

Kübler, R., Die Sagen um Merlin, 11. Aufl., 1996

Kurs in Wundern, Gutach, 2. Aufl., 1995 - Course in Miracles

Laotse, Tao te King, Diederichs, 1978

Lexikon der östlichen Weisheitslehren, Bern, 1994

Maharaj, Sri N.. ICH BIN, Bielefeld, 2. Aufl., 1992

Mecca, C., Michael Jackson - American Master, CAM Publishing, 1996

Mittwede, M., Wörterbuch Sanskrit - Deutsch, Dietzenbach, 1997

Morrison, T., Paradise, 1997

Morton, A., Lady Diana, 1997

OK Magazine, 4th April 1997

OK Magazine 11th April 1997

Redfield, J., Die Prophezeiungen von Celestine, München, 1994

Redfield, J., Die Erkenntnisse von Celestine, München, 1995

Redfield, J., Die Vision von Celestine, München, 1998

Rodrigo, L., The Avatar on Himself, Singapur

Sagan, C., Unser Kosmos, 1982

de Saint Exupéry, a., Der kleine Prinz, Düsseldorf, 1991

Saint Germain, AI AM YO SOY, Barcelona, 1991

Sathya Sai Baba, Sathya Sai Baba spricht, Band 1 - 11, Dietzenbach,

Sathya Sai Baba, Speaks, Vol. 1 -17, 1953 - 1984, Prashanti Nilayam

Sathya Sai Baba, Sai Baba erzählt, Dietzenbach, 2. Aufl., 1990

Sathya Sai Baba, Hinführung zum Höchsten Wissen - Upanishad Vahine, Dietzenbach, 1996

Sathya Sai Baba, Sanathana Sarathi, 1994, 1997-1999

Sathya Sai Briefe, Dietzenbach, 1998

Erziehung in Menschlichen Werten, Band 4: Wer bin ich?, Dietzenbach

Schmidt, K. O., In Dir Ist das LICHT, 1959

Sheldrake, R., Das Gedächtnis der Natur, Bern, 1990

Sheldrake, R., Die Wiedergeburt der Natur, 2. Aufl., 1992

Sony Europe, Presse-Mitteilung 23rd March 1999

Spalding, B.T., The Masters from the Far East, Vol. 1 - 6

Spezzano, Ch., Glücklichsein ist die beste Vergeltung, Petersberg 1996

Süddeutsche Zeitung, 28th Feb. 1998

Taraborrelli, J. R., Michael Jackson: Die Biografie, Königswinter, 1999
Tart, Ch., Transpersonale Psychologie, Olten, 1978
The Ascended Masters, Write the Book of Life, New York, 1974
Upanishaden - Die Geheimlehre der Inder, Düsseldorf, 1977
Wilber, K., Wege zum Selbst, Freiburg, 1984
Wilber, K., Eine kurze Geschichte des Kosmos, Frankfurt, 1997
Wilber, K., Eros, Kosmos, Logos, Frankfurt, 1996
Wilber, K., Vom Tier zu den Göttern, Freiburg, 1997
Wilber, K., The Eye of Spirit, Boston, 1998
Wilber, K., Naturwissenschaft und Religion, Frankfurt, 1998
Wilber, K., One Taste, Boston, 1999
Wolinks, St., Die alltägliche Trance, Freiburg, 1993
Wolinsky, St., Quantenbewusstsein, Freiburg, 1994
Zukav, G., The Seat of the Soul, New York, 1990

www.mjam.com (no longer available)
www.mjifc.com (no longer available)
www.planetjackson.com (no longer available)
www.sathyasai.org

* This was originally in English and translated to German in the 90th by myself.
Later (2014/2015) it was translated again into English by myself from the German version. After so many years the originals were lost, due to lack of my believe that I would ever need them to publish an English edition.